THE
LAST
ARROW

BOOKS BY ERWIN McMANUS

The Artisan Soul: Crafting Your Life into a Work of Art

Wide Awake: The Future Is Waiting Within You

Soul Cravings: An Exploration of the Human Spirit

The Barbarian Way: Unleash the Untamed Faith Within

Uprising: A Revolution of the Soul

Chasing Daylight: Seize the Power of Every Moment

*An Unstoppable Force: Daring to Become the Church
God Had in Mind*

ERWIN RAPHAEL McMANUS

BEST-SELLING AUTHOR OF
THE BARBARIAN WAY

THE
LAST
ARROW

SAVE NOTHING FOR THE NEXT LIFE

WATERBROOK

THE LAST ARROW

All Scripture quotations are taken from the Holy Bible, New International Version®, NIV®. Copyright © 1973, 1978, 1984, 2011 by Biblica Inc.® Used by permission. All rights reserved worldwide.

Italics in Scripture quotations reflect the author's added emphasis.

Details in some anecdotes and stories have been changed to protect the identities of the persons involved.

Hardcover ISBN 978-1-60142-953-7
eBook ISBN 978-1-60142-954-4

Copyright © 2017 by Erwin Raphael McManus

Cover design by Kristopher K. Orr; cover photography by Glen Allsop; creative direction by Aaron McManus

Published in the United States by WaterBrook, an imprint of the Crown Publishing Group, a division of Penguin Random House LLC, New York.

WATERBROOK® and its deer colophon are registered trademarks of Penguin Random House LLC.

Library of Congress Cataloging-in-Publication Data
Names: McManus, Erwin Raphael, author.
Title: The last arrow : save nothing for the next life / Erwin Raphael McManus.
Description: First Edition. | Colorado Springs, Colorado : WaterBrook, 2017. Includes
    bibliographical references.
Identifiers: LCCN 2017016087| ISBN 9781601429537 (hardcover) | ISBN
    9781601429544 (electronic)
Subjects: LCSH: Self-actualization (Psychology)—Religious aspects—Christianity. |
    Regret—Religious aspects—Christianity. | Vocation-—Christianity.
Classification: LCC BV4598.2 .M363 2017 | DDC 248.4—dc23 LC record available
    at https://lccn.loc.gov/2017016087

Printed in the United States of America
2017

10 9 8 7 6

SPECIAL SALES
Most WaterBrook books are available at special quantity discounts when purchased in bulk by corporations, organizations, and special-interest groups. Custom imprinting or excerpting can also be done to fit special needs. For information, please e-mail specialmarketscms@penguinrandomhouse.com or call 1-800-603-7051.

Like arrows in the hands of a warrior are
children born in one's youth.

—PSALM 127:4

*To my arrows: Aaron Christopher McManus, who
has never backed down from a fight, and to Mariah
McManus Goss, who is as fearless as she is fierce.*

*Long after I rest my bow and have struck my last
arrow, there will still be arrows flying true: their
names are Aaron and Mariah. The trajectories
of their lives will take them far beyond the
ground I have taken. If they were once my
arrows, they are now my archers. I dedicate this
book to them and the future they represent.*

*Aaron and Mariah: You are the tip of the spear.
You are the future. This is your fight. I pulled the
bow back as far as I could and gave you all the
strength I had to send you into flight. Fly far and
true. Cross enemy lines. Hit the mark. Set captives
free. Keep striking until the battle's won.*

—Dad

CONTENTS

Preface

THE BATTLE

It was Thursday, December 15, 2016, when I sat across from the desk of my doctor and heard him say the words we hope to never hear: "You have cancer." The signs had been there for years, but the news was still unexpected. There just isn't much you can do to prepare for that situation. The moment felt surreal to me. It was as if it were happening to someone else. I was an uncomfortable by-stander awkwardly peering into someone else's life.

What shook me into reality was to see the shock and pain in the eyes of my wife, Kim, as those words sank into her soul. Watching her made the reality of it all much too real. Sharing this news with our kids only made the pain deeper and the sorrow felt like oceans.

The doctor went on to explain that I would need an MRI and a bone scan to determine the extent of the cancer. It would need to be determined whether the cancer had spread to my bones and vital organs. The biopsy returned malignant in five of the eight areas that were tested. I was told it was important for us to move quickly. The radiation specialists informed me that surgery was our best option. Afterward we would know the process and extent of treatment.

We love Christmas, and all this fell into our lives days before our favorite holiday. It was a heavy holiday season mixed with joy and sorrow. We were all too aware of the temporary nature of life and how precious every moment is that we are given.

It was on the same day that I learned my diagnosis that I opened my manuscript to finish my final edits of this book. It could not have been incidental that the very first line I read was one I had written nearly a year earlier: "Before you hear it from someone else, I need to tell you that I'm dying."

I could not believe I was reading those words. I could not believe I wrote them. It was as if my words were written after that day's news, not before. I had to wonder if my words were more prophetic than intended. It caused me to begin to read my manuscript with a deeper and greater clarity than when I wrote it.

It seems strange to say, but I was moved by the words I had written. I spoke of life and death and what it means to live without fear or regret. I spoke as a man who knew he was going to die. Now facing the prospect of death, I only felt these words more deeply. I am writing this preface of *The Last Arrow* to tell you just that: I mean every word I have written. Even in the face of death. Especially in the face of life.

I finished this book wondering if it would be my last arrow. I know one thing for certain: I am not saving anything for the next life.

I am the pastor at Mosaic, and on the last Sunday before I went in for surgery, I gave a message that expressed my posture going forward. It was simply titled "Battle Ready." I made a decision that while cancer may define how I die, it would not define how I live.

Life is a series of challenges, adventures, and yes, even battles. There will always be giants to subdue and dragons to slay. I have already decided to die with my sword in hand. There is more courage in us than danger ahead of us. You are strong enough for the battles ahead.

My intention for this book is that you would never surrender, that you would never settle, that you would save nothing for the next life.

May you die with your quivers empty.

May you die with your hearts full.

THE POINT OF NO RETURN

William Osborne McManus married my mom when I was about three years old. He wasn't my birth father, and he never legally adopted me or my brother, but for all intents and purposes, he was the only father I ever knew. We became close, and I imagine that in my childhood, I loved him as much as any son could love a father. When I was young I called him dad. Later in life I simply called him Bill.

This man was a contradiction in every way. He was warm and engaging, charismatic and winsome. At the same time, he was a con man for whom truth was simply material woven into whatever lies he needed to tell. I remember when the movie *Catch Me If You Can,* starring Leonardo DiCaprio, came out. My brother, Alex, called me up and said, "Have you seen the movie? It's Dad." I had the exact same thought when I sat in the theater watching the movie. If you want to understand my childhood, it's summarized for you in two hours.

Over the years, Bill caused my family deep pain, callously disregarding my mom and my two little sisters, the daughters he had fathered. By the time he left us, when I was seventeen years old, all the love I had felt for him had turned to disdain. That day, he must have seen what I was feeling and thinking when he looked into my eyes, because he moved toward me aggressively. And while my instincts made me want to step back in fear, my anger made me hold my ground. Standing face to face with me, he said, "Hit me. I know you want to. See if you are man enough."

I looked at him and said, "You're not worth the effort."

He got in his car as my little sisters begged me to find a way to reconcile. I went outside to plead with him not to leave. My last memory of him from that day was seeing his face on the other side of the windshield when he clipped me with the front of the car as he drove away.

Even after that fateful day, we did find a way to reconcile and stay in touch by phone, although our contact was minimal. But there is truth to the adage that what has been torn cannot be mended. Eventually Bill remarried, and around that same time, I married as well. As if it were a script, his new wife and my wife, Kim, were pregnant at the same time. But for more reasons than I can explain, I made the hard decision of leaving my stepdad in the past and focusing on building a future for my family without Bill as part of our lives.

Before I knew it, fifteen years had passed—years in which

Bill and my son, Aaron, never met. Aaron was the first true Mc-Manus in our family. I had taken the name McManus from Bill without his ever legally becoming my father. And ironically, Mc-Manus wasn't even his name—it was an alias he assumed. He was the kind of person who was always running from his past, and his false identity was a part of that. Finally Aaron came by the name legitimately.

When Aaron was fifteen, he wanted to meet the man who gave me that name in the first place—the man I called my father. I felt I owed him that. So even though I hadn't spoken to my dad in fifteen years, I tracked him down as if he were a stranger I was trying to meet for the first time. We found him in a small town outside Charlotte, North Carolina, called Matthews. He was more than happy to see me and more than happy to meet my son. I think I had caused him great sadness by extricating myself from his life for the past fifteen years.

I didn't know what to expect, but the reunion went well enough—for a while. Then there were the last words I heard him say as we were leaving (not just the last words that day but forever, as he died not too long afterward). He said to my son in my presence, "I don't know what your dad has told you, but he was average. He was just average. His brother was exceptional, but your dad, he was just average."

Those words cut me like a knife. Please don't misunderstand me. What hurt most was not that those were the last words my father chose to say about me. Nor was I most hurt because my son heard this judgment. What cut me deepest was a terrifying sense that Bill McManus was right, that I was just average.

Frankly, if you look back at my early life, those words would have to be categorized as an exaggeration toward the positive. I was, in fact, always below average. I wasn't the C student; I was a D student. I wasn't second string; I was, at best, third string. The painful truth is that "average" had always eluded me. I seemed to always be diving toward the bottom. I was never picked first, nor second, nor anywhere in the middle. I was always literally the last player picked.

And while I always hoped that one day there would be something special about me, the truth is, I made my home in the average, if not the below average. I found a strange solace and safety in my power of invisibility and made obscurity my residence.

I am in no small part indebted to that conversation with Bill for all the thoughts that follow in this book. I do not believe anyone is born average, but I do believe that many of us choose to live a life of mediocrity. I think there are more of us than not who are in danger of disappearing into the abyss of the ordinary. The great tragedy in this, of course, is that there is nothing really ordinary about us. We might not be convinced of this, but our souls already know it's true, which is why we find ourselves tormented when we choose lives beneath our capacities and callings.

There are two ways of hearing the indictment "You are just average." One way of hearing this is as a statement of essence, that you're cut from an average cloth. The second is subtly, but significantly, different. The statement can be about character—that you have chosen a path of least resistance, that you have not aspired to the greatness that is within your grasp. Here is the painful reality: we will find ourselves defined by the average if we do not choose to defy the odds. Odds are that you and I will fall at the average. That's why it's called the average. It's where most of us live. To be above average demands a choice. It requires that we defy the odds. You have no control of whether you have been endowed with above-average talent or intelligence or physical attributes. What you can control is whether you choose to live your life defined and determined by the status quo. Even when the law of averages works against you, you can still defy the odds.

Bill's was a statement of outcome and actions. I walked away from his house that day with a clear resolve that although I have no control over whatever talent has been placed inside of me—no control over the level of my intelligence or whatever other advantages or disadvantages my genetic composition might have brought me—I will take absolute control over my personal responsibility to develop and maximize whatever potential God has given me for the good of others. The journey of *The Last Arrow* begins when you raise the bar. We need to raise the bar of our standards of our faith, of our sacrifice, of our expectations of ourselves, of our belief of the goodness and generosity of God.

We can refuse to be average. We *must* refuse to be average.

We must war against the temptation to settle for less. Average is always a safe choice, and it is the most dangerous choice we can make. Average protects us from the risk of failure, and it also separates us from futures of greatness. *The Last Arrow* is for those who decide they will never settle.

I am not talking about an uncompromising rigidity to your own expectations and standards. In fact, a huge part of the process we are about to enter into is learning how to let go of those things that don't really matter and even of those things that do not matter most. This book is not about holding others to the standards you have set. This book is about not underestimating how much God intends for your life.

I have never found a way around failure and so I cannot teach you how not to fail, but I can guide you to the place where you will never quit. Even here I feel a need to clarify. You may be doing things today that you needed to quit yesterday. There may not be anything worse than winning a battle you never should have fought. I am convinced, though, that every human being has a unique calling on his or her life—that each of us was created with intention and purpose. And I am equally certain that most of us underestimate how much God actually wants to do in our lives and through our lives. *The Last Arrow* is about leaving nothing undone that was ours to do. It is squeezing the marrow out of life. This journey is about ensuring that when we come to the end of our lives, we will arrive at our final moments with no regret.

DON'T STOP UNTIL YOU ARE FINISHED

The concept of *The Last Arrow* came to me when I was reflecting on a story from the life of the prophet Elisha in the Hebrew Scriptures. It's an obscure moment and could easily be missed, yet it is both poetic and profound. It is also, I am convinced, a window into how God works in the world and how we either open ourselves to his bigger future or ensure that we make the future smaller than he intends for us.

In this story, Jehoash is the king of Israel when the kingdoms of Israel and Judah are divided and at war against one another. His kingdom is being threatened by the armies of Amaziah, king of Judah. The one great advantage Jehoash has is that the prophet Elisha is with them, but now Elisha is suffering from an illness that will lead to his death. Jehoash goes and weeps over him, less because of his sorrow for the loss of the prophet and more because of his fear of the loss of Elisha's protection.

Jehoash calls out to Elisha, who has been a symbol and source of God's strength and power, but now is clearly at the end of his life.

Elisha then gives him a somewhat unusual series of instructions. Elisha says, "Get a bow and some arrows," and he does so. Then he tells him, "Take the bow in your hands." When Elisha commands Jehoash to do this, the king immediately complies. When the king raises the bow and arrow, Elisha puts his hands on the king's hands.

"Open the east window," he says, and the king opens it. "Shoot!" Elisha says, and Jehoash shoots. "The LORD's arrow of victory, the arrow of victory over Aram!" Elisha declares. "You will completely destroy the Arameans at Aphek."

Then he says, "Take the arrows," and the king takes them. Elisha tells him, "Strike the ground." He strikes it three times and stops. Then the Scriptures tell us something that is quite unexpected: "The man of God was angry with him and said, 'You should have struck the ground five or six times; then you would have defeated Aram and completely destroyed it. But now you will defeat it only three times.'" Right after he says this, the story tells us, "Elisha died and was buried."[1]

Much of what happens here doesn't make any sense to our modern minds. How could the king's future be so affected by whether he struck an arrow three times or five or six times? Why didn't Elisha explain to him what was required before holding him to its consequences? How could the king have known that six is the magic number and that three would leave him wanting? Up to that moment, he had done everything Elisha instructed him. But when Elisha told him to strike the ground with the arrows, the prophet left the instruction open ended.

It is not insignificant that the text says, "The man of God was angry with him." Clearly much more was happening here than meets the eye. This was no small mistake. The king began with the promise of a complete victory and afterward was the recipient of much less. And it all centers around one decision: he struck the ground three times and then stopped. Putting it another way: he quit. The Bible doesn't tell us why he quit. Maybe he was tired, maybe he felt ridiculous, maybe he thought it was beneath him, or perhaps he sensed it was an act of futility. But it is clear that, for Elisha, the fact that the king stopped striking the arrow was connected to his determination to receive the full measure of God's intention for him. He quit and the victory was lost. He just didn't want it badly enough.

I wonder how many victories are lost before the battle has even begun. I wonder how much more good God desires to usher into the world that has been thwarted by our own lack of ambition. I wonder how many times in my own life I thought I failed but actually the only thing that happened was that I quit.

What is it about us that stops before we're finished, that mistakes quitting for failure, that settles for less? I see too much of myself in this—can identify too many times when I have prayed too little, expected too little, and done too little. Have you become the kind of person who is always looking for the least you can do, trying to do only what is required? Or are you the kind of person who has given up not only on life but also on yourself? When you come to the end of your life, will you be able to say, "I gave everything I had," or will you have a hollow feeling inside of your soul that you quit too soon, that you expected too little, that you did not strike the last arrow?

I think many of us hear God say, "Take your arrows and shoot," but, much like the king, we never hear the command,

"Stop striking the ground." We simply stop before we're finished. We stop before God is finished.

There is a posture toward life that separates those who end their lives with their quivers full of untapped potential and un-seized opportunities and those who die with their quivers empty. Arrows are not meant for decor; they are meant for battle. The question each of us must answer is this: *Am I the kind of person who strikes three times and then stops, or am I the kind of person who, when commanded to strike my arrows, keeps striking and striking and striking until there are no arrows left?*

It is curious that Elisha had the king shoot the first arrow through the window and then instructed him to grab the remaining arrows and begin to strike them. We may never know the full implication of why he had him do it this way. Perhaps the arrow he shot through the window was a symbol of how God would take the victory far beyond the hand of the king. That's the way an arrow would be expected to be used. The odd command was to take the arrow and strike it instead of shoot it. It seems to imply that the focus was on what God had placed in the king's hand.

This, by the way, is the paradox of how God works in our lives. We must shoot the arrow and recognize that there are things outside our control, and we must strike the arrow and take responsibility for what is in our control. We are to shoot and strike, but what we are not to do is stop.

Most of us live our lives as if the arrows are too valuable to shoot. They look so nice inside the quiver. We may even take extra time each day to organize our arrows and make sure that they are in perfect condition. What I love about arrows, in contrast to other ancient weapons, is that while you may use a sword, it never leaves your hand, but the arrow only has value if you release it and it travels where you have not gone yourself. The arrow extends your range of impact and only fulfills its purpose when it is set into flight. We are not supposed to die with our quivers full. In fact, our greatest aspiration should be to die with our quiver empty. Those who never settle have the mind-set that they are saving nothing for the next life.

THE POINT OF NO RETURN

In 1997 I walked into a movie theater and watched an obscure film called *Gattaca*.[2] At that time, its stars (Jude Law, Ethan Hawke, and Uma Thurman) were all relatively unknown, and for most, this movie came and went without notice. But its message impacted me while I sat there in that theater, and its message has never let me go. I suspect that films have the greatest influence on us not when they pull us into their stories but when they invade our own stories.

Gattaca is the story of two brothers, Vincent and Anton. The setting is in some future time when children are genetically manipulated to be born perfect and flawless. There are, against society's best efforts, still occasionally children born called "natural babies." They are classified as invalid. The theory, of course, is that the natural human cannot compete with the one who is a result of genetic refinement.

This hits way too close to home for me. My brother, Alex, was always my contrast growing up. By the time we were in sixth grade, he was one of the fastest kids in the United States. By the time we were in high school, he was the starting and star quarterback at our school, breaking all the conference passing records. He didn't even have the decency to be a dumb jock. Instead, he did me the disservice of having an IQ that is off the scales and a natural leadership acumen that made him a general in a world of civilians. To make it easier to manage us, my mother put us both in the first grade at the same time. He was seven and I was five, and so from first grade until we graduated from high school, I operated as if I were the inferior twin.

So *Gattaca* felt like my story, the story of two brothers—one the picture of perfection, and the other a constant reminder of our flawed humanity. There is no world in which Vincent will ever surpass Anton. Anton possesses one characteristic all of us in our deepest longings wish we had as well—the absence of all of our flaws, the absence of our weaknesses, the absence of our humanity. Vincent, on the other hand, is the downgraded model of what it means to be human. He is a natural baby, and in contrast his brother is supernatural.

In the movie, the dilemma is that although Vincent is inferior, his dreams and aspirations are not limited or defined by his imperfections. His dilemma is the one all of us face. We aspire for those things that seem beyond us. Our souls seem to play a cruel joke on us, causing us to want things that seem to be impossibilities. Wouldn't it be better for all of us if we were incapable of knowing that there's more? How often is our greatest torment, that haunting thought, that the lives we long to live are not the lives we were created to live?

Yet all around us, we find hopeful reminders that seemingly ordinary people have found their way to living extraordinary lives. We know their stories; they inspire us and light afresh a flame of hope in us that we, too, might become more—that we might break through the gravitational pull of mediocrity and transcend the status quo, living a life that is uniquely our own. There does seem to be a break point, a defining moment, a moment of truth when a person decides that he or she will not settle for less, that less is no longer an option. We see this moment powerfully illustrated in the lives of these two brothers, Vincent and Anton.

Vincent has taken on an alias and is also known as Jerome. In his world, he must become someone else to become who he is. (There is no small irony in this for me, because I have lived my life with a handed-down alias, always struggling to discover who I really am.) We find the two brothers in the middle of the ocean competing to see who can swim farther. Anton is now struggling, unable to keep up with his inferior brother.

ANTON

How are you doing this, Vincent? How have you done any of this?

VINCENT

Now is your chance to find out.

(Vincent swims away a second time. Anton is forced to follow once again. Angry now, gritting his teeth, Anton calls upon the same determination we have witnessed during his constant swimming in the pool. He puts on a spurt, slowly reeling in Vincent.

Anton gradually draws alongside Vincent, certain that this effort will demoralize his older brother. But Vincent has been foxing—waiting for him to catch up. Vincent smiles at Anton. With almost a trace of sympathy, he forges ahead again. Anton is forced to go with him. They swim again for a long distance.

It is Anton who gradually becomes demoralized—his strokes weaken, his will draining away. Anton pulls up, exhausted and fearful. Vincent also pulls up. How-

ever, his face displays none of Anton's
anxiety.

They tread water several yards apart.
The ocean is choppier now. The view of the
lights on the shore is obscured by the peaks
of the waves.)

ANTON
(panic starting to show)

Vincent, where's the shore? We're too far out.
We have to go back!

VINCENT
(calling back)

Too late for that. We're closer to the other side.

(Anton looks toward the empty horizon.)

ANTON

What other side? How far do you want to go?
Do you want to drown us both?

(becoming hysterical)

How are we going to get back?!

(Vincent merely smiles back at his
younger brother, a disturbingly serene
smile.)

VINCENT

(eerily calm)

You want to know how I did it. That's how I did
it, Anton. I never saved anything for the swim
back.

These are haunting words from a person who had nothing to
lose. Maybe those of us most aware of our imperfections and flaws
are best suited for this journey. After all, what do we have to lose?
We were never supposed to amount to anything. If failure is our
inevitable future, then let's fail boldly and fail forward. But whatever happens, let's not hide behind the excuse that we didn't give
it everything we had. Perhaps the life we long for is beyond the
point of no return.

That thought has never left me: that he never saved anything
for the way back. This mind-set, I am convinced, is the funda-
mental difference between those who strike the arrow three times
and those who strike until they've used the last arrow. They leave
nothing for the way back. They save nothing for the next life.

2

Save Nothing

for the Next Life

Mick Fanning, nicknamed White Lightning, is an Australian professional surfer. Fanning won the 2007, 2009, and 2013 ASP World Tours. He seemed to have surfing in both his blood and his destiny. But on July 19, 2015, while he was at a competition in South Africa, spectators watched in horror while he fought off a shark as it tore into the rip cord on his board. Unbelievably, he escaped unhurt—but not unrattled.

Six days later he returned to surfing. Then, as if fate were determined to have its way, *another* shark pursued him and he had to get out of the water.

Frankly, if it were me, I would call it a career at that point. I would assume this was the universe's way of telling me I was no longer wanted in the ocean. But Fanning's response gives us insight into the kind of person who achieves at the highest level in his or her chosen pursuit. He said, "Surfing got me through the hardest times in my life, so to turn my back on surfing wouldn't be right."[1] In his own way, Fanning was telling us that he was saving nothing for the next life.

It makes me wonder, have I avoided the shark-infested waters of my own life and surrendered myself to standing on the shore? You don't have to be a surfer to find yourself in a perplexing dilemma and facing your greatest fears. I've joked that the two ways I have always feared dying the most are drowning and being eaten alive, which is why I have not been particularly attracted to surfing. But this I have learned over a long life: there are many ways to drown and far too many ways to be eaten alive.

We can become so afraid of death that we never live, so afraid of failure that we never risk, so afraid of pain that we never discover how strong we really are. You just have to want to ride the wave more than you fear the shark. And while South Africa is known for its shark-infested waters, I can tell you that life anywhere is no different. When we settle for less, we settle for the safety of the shore. When we resolve to never settle, we might as well recognize that the sharks are coming.

A NEVER-ENDING STORY

In 2009 I traveled to Mysore, India, to participate in the TED global community and hear some of the greatest minds in South Asia. I'll never forget the talk by Devdutt Pattanaik, an Indian physician who served as the chief belief officer of Future Group, one of India's largest retailers.[2] Pattanaik calls himself, among other things, a mythologist. He helps leverage the power of myth in business management and life. Mythology, he explains, comes from the stories, symbols, and rituals that communicate our beliefs.

I was most struck by his humorous and insightful contrast between Eastern and Western thought. His focus was on how the different myths that shape our worldviews affect us when we attempt to engage in business. But the implications go far beyond that. He contrasted the Indian mind-set, which approaches life more naturally with fuzzy logic, fluidity, and contextualization, with the Western mind-set, which is more prone toward facts, logic, and standardization. He pointed out that Hindus believing in reincarnation are not in a hurry, as they believe they have many lives to get things done, which is in contrast to the ancient Greeks, who believed that each person had only one life and, because of this, had a greater sense of urgency. When you have only one life, you have a greater sense of determination and even desperation to accomplish something meaningful. Pattanaik wasn't advocating the rightness of either view; he was simply stating a fact that how we view our existence has a radical effect on our engagement in this life.

Although there is much I admire about Eastern thought, I prefer the effect of what Pattanaik would call Western mythology. I wake up every day with an overwhelming conviction that this life matters and that we each get one life and one life only to make a mark in history. I am absolutely convinced that what we do in this life matters and that time is our most precious commodity. It's kind of frustrating, when you think about it. If this life matters so much, it seems unfair that we don't get a warm-up life to prepare us for the real one. There are no trial runs. In that sense, life does not allot us do-overs. Once we have taken our last breaths, our stories in history have been written. And although we have stories that continue in eternity, it is imperative that we understand that these stories begin in the here and now.

Pattanaik summarized Western versus Eastern mythologies by giving one keyword for each worldview. For him, it was a contrast between a Western *one* and an Eastern *infinity*. The Greeks, again, were convinced they each had only one life, and that worldview compelled them to aspire to live their most heroic lives. The Hindu mind sees our existence as infinite and would be more compelled by the connectedness of all things.

Seeing the contrast between these two worldviews helps me understand the power of the Hebraic mind-set. At the intersection of Western and Eastern worldviews, the Hebrews were compelled by both the one and the infinite. We each have one life, but this life has eternal significance. What we do in this one life has infinite implications, and beyond that, our stories are bigger than history. Our stories don't end when we do. They are only the beginning of much greater stories, the content of which we are completely unaware. So in that sense we get the best of both worlds. Our deepest meaning must go beyond that which is confined to time and space, yet that does not in any way diminish the importance of this moment. If the urgency of one life is what compels us to live our most heroic lives, then let's make the most of this one life each of us has. At the same time, we can only live that most heroic life well when we have a deep sense of connectedness to that which is infinite and eternal.

WHEN REALITY HITS

It was an evening like so many evenings: uneventful, calm, and peaceful. I was lying in bed and Kim was in the shower washing off the exhaustion of the day. Everything seemed so serene, until I heard a crash coming from behind the bathroom door. Sometimes a sound tells you more than you want to know. I didn't see anything that happened, but I immediately knew that Kim had suffered a bad fall. And if the sound was communicating accurately, her head had cracked against the marble floor.

I jumped out of bed and rushed into the bathroom and saw her lying on the floor. She was definitely dazed and confused and obviously in a great deal of pain. If I remember correctly, she asked me to help her up, or maybe I asked her if I could help her up. It's all a little blurry to me. What I do remember is that the moment I tried to help her up, I saw a large pool of blood behind her head and realized it was better to keep her lying down. She tried to get to her feet, but I insisted she lie still and not look around. I did not want her to see how much blood had come out of her head.

In my panic I grabbed the phone to call 911 for help, punching in the numbers as fast as I could. You cannot imagine my surprise when a voice answered on the other side in an automated voice, "AT&T directory assistance. May I help you?" I had never called 911 before, and the lack of urgency wasn't what I was expecting. I think it was Kim who pointed out that I had dialed 411 and that I needed to call 911.

It's strange how much those 911 moments reveal who we are. I will just confess right up front: seeing Kim lying in a pool of blood sent me into disarray. She calls it panic; I call it love.

There was a cultural moment when I felt as if our whole nation dialed 911. It was September 11, 2001.

Like so many others, I remember exactly where I was and what I was doing when the two planes crashed into the towers of the World Trade Center and sent our country into crisis. I was driving to the Los Angeles International Airport when I received a call from my family imploring me not to get on the plane I was about to board and to please come home. Honestly, they didn't make any sense to me at all. They were talking about a plane crashing into a building in New York, and although it sounded tragic, I did not understand the implications of what was going on. When the second plane careened into the second tower, the picture of what was happening became clearer.

I am convinced that many of us have been marked by that day and that, as a result of it, either consciously or unconsciously, many of us have made decisions that have altered the course of our values, decisions, and even lives. Two specific things happened for me because of 9/11. First, it convinced me that I should become an American citizen. I was born in El Salvador, and on 9/11 I was still a Salvadorian citizen and only a permanent resident in the United States. Deciding to become a citizen of this country was my way of saying that this loss was my loss, this wound was my wound, and that whatever future needed to come out of this tragedy, I was committed to being a part of it regardless of the consequence or the cost.

The second was a sudden increase in opportunities to speak across North America. There came quickly after 9/11 an aftershock that affected my life personally. Speakers began to withdraw from events they had committed to. Many of the organizations holding the events were already financially committed, so they had to find quick replacements for their preferred speakers. It began with one call, and then another. Soon I was getting an unexpected number of requests. Somehow the word got out that I would get on any plane at any time to anywhere, or to summarize: I had a callous disregard for my own personal well-being and life. I was flooded with invitations. I was replacing the biggest names in the speaking space. Many of them were well known for their messages of faith, courage, and risk, but under these circumstances, they felt it was better to cancel and not get on a plane. It would be nice to believe that I was the preferred speaker at all those events, but I am actually quite comfortable with the truth that I was pretty much the only one available.

It got to a point where my wife started getting angry because she felt the danger of the choices we were making. Our kids were young, and it was no small thing for Kim to consider that she might be raising our children alone.

I remember one particular day when a renowned speaker canceled at another event and I was called that day and asked to come that week and replace him. I sat down with Kim and said, "I am flying across the country to speak."

In frustration she asked me which speaker had canceled this time. I asked her why she wanted to know, and she said, "I want to call his wife and tell her that her husband is a coward."

Sometimes we forget that people respond differently to trauma. At the same time, it is those moments when we are confronted with the uncertainty of life that allow us to see ourselves most clearly. Even as I write these words, I am a few hours away from learning the results of a recent biopsy. But I am convinced of this: you must not allow fear to steal your future, and every day that you walk this earth you must make sure you save nothing for the next life. You must never allow fear to keep you grounded. The moment you choose to play it safe, you've lost the game. Instead of running from your fears, lean into them, for on the other side of them is the future you long for. These moments form character and forge the future.

What I call "9/11 moments" are those times when there is a clear line of distinction between fear and faith. I wish I could tell you that I never felt the grip of fear while I was on those planes, but I did. There were more occasions than I want to remember when I felt overwhelmed with the possibility of that day being the last time I would see my wife and kids. Let me tell you, the way you kiss your family good-bye when you wonder if it could be the last time is so different than all those days you assume you have one more day to live. Sitting on a plane, I would take a deep breath, talk to God, and repeat in my heart, *Today is a good day to die*, which might explain why I have so much admiration for the culture of the samurai. The samurai lived to serve their master with both their life and their death. The word *samurai* literally means "servant" and interestingly enough can also be translated "deacon." Perhaps their most powerful virtue was that they saw no tragedy in death, only in not living a life of service to their master. Avoiding death is not the same as pursuing life. I am convinced that it is only when we put death behind us that we can genuinely live life to the fullest.

If 9/11 taught me anything, it was to save nothing for the next life, to do what must be done, to say what must be said, to write the words that must be written, and to live the life that must be lived. Time seduces us into believing that it is the one friend who will never run out on us, but the cruel truth is that it always does. It would not be unfair to say that time lies to us. It tricks us into believing that we can wait until tomorrow to do the thing we should have done yesterday. And while I find an endless number of reasons why people leave things in this life undone, I find one unifying characteristic of those who leave nothing for the next life: a sense of urgency.

THE POWER OF NOW

Urgency can be fueled by many things: passion, conviction, even compassion. But often I find that urgency, in its rawest form, is fueled by desperation. The shift that happens when you refuse to remain or be defined by the average comes when you cross a line others would consider madness. While everyone around you says it can wait, you know it can't. I find that we are often more comfortable speaking about passion than about urgency, but it is urgency that gives our passions deadlines. Passion is about what fuels us; urgency is about how much it matters right now. The most important things in life rarely come with urgency. It may seem counterintuitive, but the most important things in life are most easily pushed to the back burner. The urgent is rarely the most important; but the most important must always be the most urgent. The most important things in life require that you bring your own urgency. Passion is the fuel that brings urgency. Leadership is about bringing urgency to the things that matter most.

The Last Arrow isn't about what you can do or could do; it's about what you must do. It's not about maximizing your potential or achieving your personal greatness; it's about being consumed with an importance and urgency that are bigger than us. Rare are those who allow themselves to be consumed by things that are bigger than they. And though the shift from unconsumed to consumed is subtle, it is seismic. Those people know that it is out of their hands if the plane lands, but it's completely in their hands if they are on the plane when it takes off. They decide that if God has placed the arrows in their hands, they will strike them until they can strike no more. If one day we are to have a conversation with God about the measure of our lives, I would rather have him ask me why I tried to do too much than have him ask me why I settled for so little.

Though the prophet Elisha was the agent of the exchange, the future was literally placed in King Jehoash's hands by God himself. God's desire was to give the king complete victory; he instead settled for a life of endless battles. It is not coincidental that Scripture says, "The man of God was angry with him and said, 'You should have struck the ground five or six times.'"[3]

You'll be hard pressed to find any story in the Scriptures in which God becomes angry because someone has too much faith, too much determination, too much resolve. The truth is, we keep repeating the same mistakes over and over again. God puts the bow and the arrows in our hands and tells us to shoot and to strike. And instead of pressing the limits of what God could do in and through our lives, we assume that his intention for us is less and so we settle for what we can do rather than what God intended to do through us.

The reality is that all of us settle in some areas of our lives, and that settling is an inevitable part of even the most successful enterprise. Even the Scriptures encourage us to settle conflicts and, in fact, to learn the skill of settling conflicts without the need for courts or judges to accomplish anything meaningful in life. You have to know where you need to settle and where you should never settle. One of the nuanced skills of people who maximize their capacity and optimize their impact on the world is that they know which battles not to fight. They know which ground to give up. They know where to settle. This is not because they're postured for compromise; it's because they have a clarity about what really matters to them. They know what their lives are about. They have profound intention, and that intention informs every arena of their lives. Those who care about everything actually care about nothing.

The Last Arrow is not a call to never settle in every arena in life; *The Last Arrow* is a call to never settle about what God intends to do with your life. You have to know what matters; you have to know who you are; you have to know what your life is to be given to. For in the end, the one thing where you must never settle for less is the calling that God has on your life, the purpose for which he has created you, the impact he designed you to make in the world.

The great tragedy that I have witnessed over and over again is that we keep underestimating how much God wants to do in us and through us. Too many of us have believed the lies we have been told: that we're not good enough, we're not smart enough, we're not talented enough, we're just not enough. One of the facets of God that makes him extraordinary is his ability to do the impossible through ordinary, everyday, common people like you and me. This book has one intention: that whether you win or lose, succeed or fail, live a life of celebrity or anonymity, that when you take your last breath, you will know without reservation that you have given everything you have, everything you are, to the life you have been entrusted with.

When my kids were young, we had a family saying. Well, it was more of a mantra, really. In those moments when they were tired and discouraged or felt inadequate for the task, we would say, "McManuses never give up."

Maybe even as you are turning the pages of this book, you know deep within you that you gave up on your best life a long time ago. You gave up believing that God would do great things in your life. Maybe you have given up believing that tomorrow can be better than today. Maybe you have given up on love or on hope or on joy or on meaning. Whatever it may be that you once believed in so deeply, somehow the hardships and heaviness of life stole it from your soul. You thought God gave up on you, but deep down inside, you know it was you who gave up on God.

Is it possible that failure is simply the result of giving up too soon? Is it possible that our most tragic failure is giving up on ourselves? This is the paradox of our spiritual journeys. When we put our complete trust in God, it places upon us greater responsibility, not less. Even when the victory is the Lord's, we are still called to be the warriors in the midst of the battle.

It should shake you to the core that God wanted to give King Jehoash a complete victory and that all he needed the king to do was strike an arrow five or six times until he was instructed to stop. Maybe all God was looking for was someone who wouldn't quit. Maybe all he ever needs is someone who refuses to give up.

Is it possible that God is waiting to do more than we could ever ask or imagine and is looking throughout the earth for someone who refuses to settle? Maybe it's time for you to pick up your bow, grab your arrows, and begin to strike. After all, what's the point of saving your arrows? You can't take them with you after you have taken your last breath. You have one life to use everything you have been entrusted with, so you might as well save nothing for the next life.

3

Choose the Future

In 1958 Alby Cardona must have felt the weight of the world on her shoulders. She was barely twenty years old and had two boys both under age two and an alcoholic husband from whom she'd had to flee to safety. Making the best of her circumstances, she found a job at the InterContinental Hotel just outside of the capital of El Salvador. She worked as a restaurant hostess for what at the time was a world-class hotel, and after putting in endless hours, she would bring home about a hundred dollars a month.

This was not the life she had expected nor the life anyone else would have expected for her. Beautiful and brilliant, she had once thought that the sky was the limit for her. Then, in an unexpected twist, at the age of sixteen, she fell in love with her language professor at the private school she attended and soon married him.

On the surface they looked like the perfect couple. He was handsome and brilliant and spoke multiple languages. He seemed the perfect match for her. As you can imagine, they were married against her parents' wishes, but frequently those kinds of choices are difficult to understand until the curtain is pulled back to expose there is much more going on. Often people perceive us as running to something when in fact we're running from something else. At the age of sixteen, my mom saw marriage as her only way of escape from a family life that became for her untenable. She had always loved her parents, but she grew up in a different time, when strictness oftentimes crossed the line of severity. Unfortunately, she found herself moving from a difficult situation into a dangerous one. Her parents were strict, but soon she discovered that her husband was unsafe. Evidently my dad was a brilliant and wonderful man except when he began to drink. He was an abusive alcoholic, and my mom quickly became the victim of domestic violence.

One morning, while Alby was working at the restaurant, a businessman who said he worked for Pan Am approached her in a mildly flirtatious manner. He noted that she was extremely attractive and would look great in a Pan Am uniform. If you know anything of Pan Am's history, they were renowned for their beautiful stewardesses and their high commitment to appearance and attractiveness. He told her that if she was interested in becoming a Pan Am stewardess, she should come see him in his hotel room on the seventh floor. She was polite but had no intention of taking him up on his offer. She assumed it was nothing more than a pickup line and that he was simply trying to seduce her with opportunity.

Several hours later, when the day was winding down, one of

her girlfriends came by the restaurant. Alby, surprised to see her, asked her what she was doing there on her day off. She responded enthusiastically, "Haven't you heard? Pan Am is here interviewing for stewardesses. They are taking interviews on the seventh floor."

In that moment, my mom realized she had misinterpreted the man's intentions and that perhaps the most important opportunity of her life was about to slip away. She ran up to the seventh floor, where the executive from Pan Am was already packed and leaving his room. When he saw her, he said he'd thought she did not have any interest in the job. She responded that she was very interested in it. All the application forms had already been filled, so he took out several blank sheets of paper and told her to simply sign them and he would take care of the rest.

Before she knew it, she had received an offer from Pan Am. A new career in a new country was what they offered, but she knew it was more than that: it was a new future and a new life.

My mom's parents were strongly patriarchal. There was no way she could take this opportunity without the approval of her father. It didn't matter that she was already married, out of the house, and on her own. In Latin culture, one still needed permission from the Don. She would also certainly need her parents' help if she was going to seize the opportunity to create a new future for not only herself but also for her two boys. Her mother was more than willing to fill the gap of caring for her children until she could bring them to the States, but her father was adamant that she was not to leave the country and would not support her in this new endeavor. His disapproval meant she would lack the financial resources to move to the States and begin a new life.

As far as she could see, this obstacle was insurmountable, until one day while she was at work, the chef who ran the restaurant inquired if she was going to accept the opportunity with Pan Am. She explained that although she wanted to take on this new challenge, it just wasn't possible. She was unable to finance her move from San Salvador to Miami on her own and therefore would have to miss out on this opportunity.

The chef had come to care about this young woman who worked so hard. He was from Switzerland, and it would have been easy for him to be an observer in the struggles of the people around him rather than involve himself in their lives. But when he heard her story, he told her that she needed to go—that she needed to take the risk to leave everything she knew and go into this new unknown.

To her surprise, the next time they saw each other, he handed her a wallet with $250, which for her was more than two months' salary. He handed her this gift and told her, "Now you need to go." The money he gave her was worth far more than $250. Its greatest value was not in currency; the gift he gave her was far deeper and more profound than that. This man became for her the voice that gave her permission to leave her past behind and go create a better future.

When my mom got on that plane and left me and my brother in the arms of our grandparents, it might have seemed that she was leaving us behind. But she wasn't leaving us; she was leaving *for* us. She set her past on fire so that she could create a new future. After leaving us in San Salvador, my mom lived in Miami and San Francisco and New York. I remember as a small child pointing at the airplanes and saying, "There's my mom."

I find that many of us keep longing for a new future while holding on to the past. We desperately want God to create something new for us, but we refuse to let him tear away all the old from us. Somehow I think it is not incidental that my mom's name, Alby, literally means "dawn." She's had a lot of dark nights but somehow always finds herself rising up when the morning comes. I'll confess that it was not easy for me as a child to understand many of the choices she needed to make, yet the one thing I have learned from her is that if you live in the past you die to your future.

KISS YOUR PAST GOOD-BYE

If we are not careful, our future will simply be an extension of our past. There is a natural domino effect from the moments behind us to the moments in front of us. However, only when life is least disruptive do we enjoy this kind of predictability and continuity. But the moments that will actually define us, the moments that will carry the greatest weight in our lives, the moments that will create for us the future we've always longed for, are not those moments that easily integrate into our past, but instead they are the disruptive moments, the moments when we must choose between extending our past and creating our future. The prophet Elisha understood this well.

Long before the arrow-striking scene we looked at earlier, before Elisha had begun his prophetic career, he was having what I imagine was a day much like every other day, plowing his fields with his oxen. He was being faithful to the life he had been given. Perhaps only in his deepest thoughts and secret desires did he imagine his life would ever change. Then in the afternoon, everything changes for him. When Elisha has the taste of dust in his mouth and is caked in sweat and feeling the exhaustion that comes from manual labor, the older prophet Elijah unexpectedly comes to him and throws his cloak around him as a symbol that he has chosen him, or more accurately that God has chosen him to be his next prophet.

Elisha leaves the oxen and runs after Elijah, and understanding the full implications of what has just happened, he bids him, "Let me kiss my father and mother goodbye . . . and then I will come with you."

Elijah responds in a somewhat obscure and coy way, saying to him, "Go back. . . . What have I done to you?"[1] Elijah doesn't explain anything. He merely puts the cloak around Elisha and walks away.

There is a parallel between what Elijah does not say to Elisha here and what Elisha does not say to King Jehoash in the arrow-striking story we've already looked at.[2] The important point not to miss here is that no one can tell you your future. You have to decide what future you want, what future you will pursue, what future you must create. For Elisha, this is a defining moment when he leaves his past to go and find his future.

After he has kissed his father and mother good-bye, he literally sets his past on fire. He takes his yoke of oxen and slaughters them. He cuts the wooden plowing equipment to pieces and uses them to cook the meat. He gives the meat to all the people, and they eat and celebrate. Then after everything he used to have is only dust and ashes, he sets out to follow Elijah and become his servant.

For Elisha, this wasn't a turn from wrong to right or evil to good but rather from the life he had to the life he was offered. Elisha's extreme action was both his declaration and his determination that there was no turning back. If in a few weeks or months or even years things were not going as he had hoped, if Elijah did not prove to be a man worth aligning with, or if the future became more difficult than he had imagined, there was nothing to return to. There were no plows or oxen waiting for him at home, no previous life waiting for him to pick up where he left off. Other than as a memory, the past was no longer available to him. He had only one direction—forward.

As long as we have a contingency plan to go backward, then backward is where we will find ourselves going in the end. For too many of us, our plan B is to go back to the life we never wanted in the first place. Isn't that exactly what happened to Israel when they had finally found their deliverance from Egypt? They cried out to God to be free and then complained to him when he granted their request. All they wanted was to be delivered from Egypt, and then later all they wanted was to be delivered back to Egypt again.

If slavery remains an option, we will find ourselves abdicating our freedom. We just don't usually call it slavery. We call it safety. We call it comfort. We call it security. We call it responsibility.

I'm not saying you shouldn't have a plan B or a plan C or a plan D. What I am saying is that all your alternative plans need to be oriented toward the future and not stuck in the past. It's not that those who settle for less don't want more for their lives; it's that they want the "more" where they are and are not willing to go where the "more" is waiting for them. Yet over and over again, we find that God presses against us and forces us to choose.

While Abraham was still in Mesopotamia, God spoke to him and said, "Leave your country and your people . . . and go to the land I will show you."[3] One of the inescapable themes of the Scriptures is that we cannot grab hold of the future if we keep holding on to the past. This in some ways is a paradox that we are called into as followers of Christ. A singular event in history changes everything for humanity's future. What Jesus did two thousand years ago is a call not to live in the past but to create the future. In fact, this is the central narrative of what it means to be a follower of Jesus.

Luke tells us that Jesus had a series of encounters as he and his disciples were walking down a road:

A man said to him, "I will follow you wherever you go."

Jesus replied, "Foxes have dens and birds have nests, but the Son of Man has no place to lay his head."

He said to another man, "Follow me."

But he replied, "Lord, first let me go and bury my father."

Jesus said to him, "Let the dead bury their own dead, but you go and proclaim the kingdom of God."

Still another said, "I will follow you, Lord; but first let me go back and say goodbye to my family."

Jesus replied, "No one who puts a hand to the plow and looks back is fit for service in the kingdom of God."[4]

With that last reference to the plow, Jesus seemed to be alluding to Elisha. With different nuances, he gave each of his would-be followers the same answer: set your past on fire. *You cannot follow me into the future if you are holding on to your past.* To be clear, there may be things from your past that go with you into the future; you just have to leave behind your past and those who choose to remain there.

WHERE LIFE IS GOING

Peter followed Jesus into his future, and his brother, Andrew, was right there with him. John did the same, and his brother, James, was always at his side; they became known as the "sons of thunder." It is always harder to journey into the future alone and always better when you are able to do it with those who have chosen it as well. Sometimes you have to leave those who are a part of your past so that you may create a future for them as well. Still, sometimes you have to say good-bye. There have been times when I have held on to my past for far too long and treated it as if it were my future. Sometimes it's more about the things you can't let go of, and other times it's about the things you can't seem to get a hold of. It would be so much easier if God met us in a vacuum. It would be much less complicated if our lives weren't already full and entangled in our pasts when God was calling us into new futures.

When I came to faith, I was about twenty years old and had been dating the same person for two years. She was a wonderful woman who probably should not have been dating me. For the first two years of our relationship, she was the person of faith and I was the one without a faith at all. She went to church regularly and lived a life that was admirable and inspiring even to me. She always wanted me to believe but didn't really know how to get me there.

Then unexpectedly I had a life-changing encounter with Jesus Christ that changed everything for me. At first she was thrilled that we could now share in our faith together. What threw her off guard was how intense my faith became so quickly. She was a good person with a sincere but low-temperature faith. You know the old adage "Be careful what you pray for." I know she prayed that I would meet God. I also know that it was my meeting God that eventually ended our relationship. We dated for another two years, trying to find a new rhythm in our relationship. Strangely, it had been easier for us to date when I didn't believe.

I have never been a temperate person when it comes to convictions. I am either all in or all out. In the areas that actually matter, moderation is not an option for me. Four years into our relationship, the two of us were standing in a parking lot at the University of North Carolina at Chapel Hill. We could feel our relationship unraveling. I will never forget how exasperated she was when she looked at me and said, "I feel like I am trying and you're not. I am trying to find a compromise, and you seem unwilling." Then she asked the question that clarified everything for me. She said, "I know the world needs Jesus, but why do you have to take on that responsibility? Why can't you meet me halfway? Why can't you compromise on this?"

It was then I knew that, while we had a past together, we did not have a future. I felt such sadness when I realized that she was exactly right. And standing in that parking lot, I looked at her for the last time and said, "You're right. You have been trying to compromise, and I realize that in this I cannot. I can't meet you halfway. I can't compromise at all. This is what my life is now and where my life is going."

When I walked away that day, I knew I had just set my past on fire. Frankly, it's not easy to walk away from a person you love and just as difficult to walk away from someone who loves you.

Maybe this is one of the biggest reasons many of us settle for less. We do not believe there is love waiting for us in the future. We are afraid that if we leave something behind in our past, there is not something better waiting for us in the future.

I've always been uncomfortable with the words of Jesus when he turned to the crowd and said to them, "If anyone comes to me and does not hate father and mother, wife and children, brothers and sisters—yes, even their own life—such a person cannot be my disciple."[5] Jesus was never uncomfortable with hyperbole, and in fact, he understood that the language of exaggeration would be needed for us to understand the extreme cost in pursuing the life he was calling us into. Jesus chose this language to create a visceral understanding of what it means to love God with all of your being. It is inescapable that you will be forced to choose between God and everything you hold dear. What he is saying is that there are people in your life who would keep you trapped in the past, and you have to be willing to let them go so that you can move into your future.

Sometimes, though, it's not the people who keep us in the past; it's our own sense of identity.

THE FUTURE OF SUCCESS

The past is more than what we've done or where we've been; it's who we are. Elisha was a farmer. This is what he knew. This is what he was good at. It was his guaranteed success. The life he was being called to was fraught with uncertainty, instability, and even danger.

There is a subtle difference between your identity being rooted in your essence and your identity being rooted in your success. What you do comes out of who you are, but who you are must exist apart from what you do. If your identity is rooted in your success, then you will lose who you are when failure comes your way.

Recently, after speaking at a conference, I was invited to participate in a live interview. I was asked how I have dealt with success now that I'd been invited to speak at this conference. (It's funny how, even when we say we believe in character above talent and in faithfulness over the spectacular, there is still a not-very-subtle belief that it was speaking to thousands that validated my life and not the choices I made that remain unseen by most.) I told the interviewer that I thought I was successful when I was completely unknown and working with only a handful of people and that I never saw the measure of my success as speaking in large venues or conferences.

Success is a tyrant that will enslave you just as quickly as failure. If you let success own you, you will find yourself trapped by your success and terrified by the possibility of failure. Success will lie to you and tell you that your future is just an extension of your past, when at its best, success is simply preparation for new challenges. Every day you will have to choose between living in the past, staying in the present, or creating a future. The great danger lies in that the easy path is to hold on to what you know, cling to what you have, and make the future an extension of the past. Though there is no way to stop time, you have to choose the future. Although you are grounded in the past, you must not be grounded *by* the past. And while tomorrow is coming regardless of what you do, the future comes *because* of what you do.

More than a decade ago, when I wrote *Chasing Daylight,*[6] I discovered that one of the most obvious things I wrote became one of the most controversial, but I think it's worth repeating. The most spiritual thing you will do today is to choose. And whether you realize it or not, every choice you make has an effect on your future. In fact, the choices you make are the material from which the future is made. If our best futures can be known only in the mind of God, then how critical is it that we hear his voice and heed his call. God is never calling us into the past; he is always calling us into the future. When he calls us to choose him, he is calling us to choose the future as well. This process is far more painful than can be described by words. Sometimes the future demands all of us and all from us. We will all find ourselves at some point in our lives being asked to put everything we know on an altar with only a promise of a future we do not know. And like every sacrifice after the altar has been built, we have to set it on fire. It's no different when the future calls us. It is in that moment where we have to set our past on fire to receive a future awaiting us.

4

SET YOUR PAST ON FIRE

In 1977 our family's home in Raleigh, North Carolina, erupted in an electrical fire, which consumed everything inside and left us with a hollow shell for a home. I'll never forget the smell of the smoke after the fire destroyed everything we considered valuable. I also will never forget what I saw over the mantel of our fireplace, for there the trophies that had adorned our family room were now indistinguishable pieces of melted metal. It was no big tragedy that all of my participation trophies were lost. It was more serious that all my brother's incredible awards, which once were our family's symbols of honor and celebration, were melted together.

I watched my mom as she lamented our loss, and she kept saying over and over again to my brother, "We'll fix these. We'll fix these. We'll find a way to replace them."

My brother seemed strangely unmoved. I don't remember exactly what he said, but I remember the insight I walked away with: *If those trophies are the highlights of our lives, then our lives were not worth living, going forward.* Those trophies were the past, and it would be a waste of our time and effort to try to reclaim the past. It would be much better for us to focus on creating the future.

I have seen far too many people live in the glories of their past successes. Sometimes that's all they can talk about. They are trapped in 1976 or 1988 or 1994. So in a strange way, I am grateful for that electrical short behind the refrigerator. If I had any inclination to live in the past, that moment brought it to a close. Perhaps in the grand scheme of things I had not yet learned to set my past on fire, yet out of those ashes I began to create a new and better future. My future would not be an extension of my past. My plows and oxen were gone, and it was time to move into a new future.

Sometimes to set your past on fire means to break free from the expectations of others. Far too often we live our lives being what others want us to be rather than who we are supposed to be. There is a difference, of course, between setting the past on fire and burning bridges. It's a dangerous thing to burn bridges we might have to cross again. The advice from Scripture to be at peace with all men if at all possible is the best posture with which to live our lives. So before we move on, let me give you this warning: be careful where you set fires. Burning bridges is about setting other people on fire, which is not recommended. This chapter is about burning away everything that should remain in your past and not be taken into your future.

PLAYING WITH FIRE

Scott Reynolds has been my friend for more than twenty years, and I have had the privilege of watching the evolution of both his life as a person and his life as a professional. Scott is a great husband and an amazing father, and there isn't a better family to model one's life after. When people meet his wife, Amy, and their children, Zane and Audrey, they're immediately drawn into the warmth and kindness of their tight-knit family. Others might even be caught a bit off guard when they realize that Scott has been the producer and writer on such shows as Netflix's *Iron Fist* and *Jessica Jones* and Showtime's *Dexter.* Hard to imagine that his career path began as a writer's assistant on *Touched by an Angel,* yet Scott might never have lived out his award-winning writing career had he not set his past on fire.

In what must have seemed to be another life, Scott was a student at a small Christian college in Tennessee. It was on that all-important day when prospective students visit the school with their parents that Scott decided to start a fire—literally—and burn his college career to the ground. A fence stood between him and the oncoming parents and high-school seniors, and Scott decided to set the fence on fire and scream from the other side, "Help me! Get me out of here! I'm trapped in hell." This might have been a foreshadowing of his soon-to-come career as a writer on *Dexter. Dexter,* for those of you who are unaware, was a show about a serial killer whose moral compass allowed him to kill only serial killers. What was certain was that his actions that day set him on the path to getting expelled. Knowing Scott, I'd say he could have just decided the prank was funny enough to risk the consequences. But whether conscious or unconscious, he actually was trapped and made a decision to burn a bridge to which he could never return.

I'm not recommending that you set your past on fire literally. Let's leave that for the Scott Reynoldses of the world. But like Scott, if you want a different life, you have to give up the one you have. There are things and even people you will have to leave behind if you are going to keep moving forward. What's wonderful is that you never have to leave behind the people whom you love and who are for you. Quite often the resources of the past provide the material to build the future, but you have to leave behind those things that you love and even people you care about who would keep you trapped in the past and would rob from you the future God has for you.

But be careful while you are pretending to set your past on fire, that it's not actually your future you are burning to the ground. Setting your past on fire is not about self-destructive behavior. In fact, it is quite the opposite. It is about making the hard decisions to leave behind that which would steal from you the future God intends for you.

The journey into our best future always passes through the furnace. The fire both forges us into who we must become and frees us to live the lives for which we were created. This of course leads us to an important warning: do not confuse setting your past on fire with burning bridges you may need to cross one day. Elisha made an altar of his past as an offering to God. It was his way of saying, "I will never turn back from the calling you have placed on my life." As painful as it may be, there are times when we leave behind both people and opportunities that we care deeply about. Burning bridges is a different thing. We burn bridges when we take people for granted and demean their value in our lives.

Always make sure that you do the right thing in the right way. To set your past on fire is not the same as choosing a scorched-earth strategy. It's about letting go of those things that have a hold on you. Do not lose sight of the fact that just because it's time to move forward, the things in the past did not have great value for that time in your life. Appreciate the past, but live in the present and for the future.

I sat with one of my closest friends in my car outside my house. We had one of those long conversations that probably didn't last as long as it felt. He was using shrouded language, but his intentions were clear. After more than thirty years of marriage, and nearly as long as a pastor, he kept talking about his future as if it were a choice between his freedom and his character. I could hear between every word that he had already decided in his heart to leave his wife. He was trying to justify how he could never fulfill his dreams, achieve his potential, and even be the leader God wanted him to be if he could not be free to start over again. Although he would repeatedly deny it, time revealed he had already established an inappropriate relationship with another woman. And even after this proved to be true, he still felt completely justified and was even incredulous that any of us could hold his choices against him. The tragedy of course is that his decisions caused so much pain to so many people and in the end did not give him the life he longed for.

I have seen too many people I care about end up making choices that leave them like Nero setting Rome on fire. God's future will never come to us at the cost of our character. This person that I once respected so much made the tragic mistake of leaving in his past what should have been his future and making his future what should have been his past. He chose to keep what was never his and leave behind that which had been entrusted to him. So let me be clear: Elisha took the plows and the oxen and built an altar. He set everything on fire that was no longer his to keep. He did this not to create a future of his own making but to enable him to receive the future that God was creating for him.

THE FUTURE OF THE PAST

Sometimes setting your past on fire is less walking away from it than rising above it.

For the past ten years, my wife, Kim, has made trips to Bangladesh, one of the most impoverished, dangerous, and dark places in the world. On a few of those trips, our daughter, Mariah, has gone as well. Mariah's first trip to Bangladesh was when she was only nineteen years old. I'll admit right up front that I was uncomfortable enough that my wife would go to Bangladesh with a team of women; it was even harder for me when my daughter went, leading a team of young girls herself. They went to a place known as Banishanta, which is essentially nothing more than a village built around a huge number of seaport brothels. There is basically one form of commerce, one source of income: prostitution. If this were not bad enough, Banishanta is surrounded by the poverty and violence that Bangladesh has become known for. Since the 1970s, up to thirty million people have been displaced, gone missing, or been killed. It seems that human trafficking either exists under the radar or is covered by a callous indifference.

Kim and Mariah fell in love with the women who ran a particular work known as Alingon. Through the Alingon home, a small number of girls have been saved from lives of prostitution and abuse. It's not something we think of often, but prostitutes have children, and when those children are daughters, they become commodities in the world of human trafficking. These girls are basically harvested for the sex trade: born out of prostitution, born into prostitution. The problem is so big, so overwhelming, that it might cause most who are moved with concern to feel that nothing can be done, but one mother and daughter decided they would do whatever they could do.

Before I met Rose Mary Banerjee and her youngest daughter, Maryline Banerjee Rimpa, I had some assumptions about why they were doing what they were doing. I never questioned the nobility of their mission or the integrity of their intent, but I assumed that—unlike Kim and Mariah, who could move in and out of those worlds—Bangladesh was the only world Rose Mary and Maryline knew. But when I met Rose Mary, I realized she was a highly intelligent woman who could have easily left Bangladesh and chosen a different life, as she had family across the world. I asked her why she decided to stay in Bangladesh and, in particular, give her life to Banishanta. She was quick to respond that yes, she could live anywhere else, but she knew that by staying in her country, she could do the most good. Rose Mary is a wonderful reminder that the way forward is not a way out or a way of escape; it is a way into the lives that God has called us to.

Because of Rose Mary and Maryline, today dozens of girls are receiving free educations, experiencing healthy environments, and perhaps for the first time in their lives, finding the healing power of love and hope and faith. It's almost more than I can wrap my head around that the daughters of prostitutes will one day become teachers and doctors and perhaps even prime ministers. Wouldn't it be an interesting twist to the story if a young girl from Banishanta could one day rise to lead her own country and end the horrific practice of human trafficking?

Sometimes your future will call you to stand right in the middle of your past. The difference, of course, is that you are not defined by the past, enslaved by the past, or held captive by it. Sometimes the only way to set people free from the past is to create a different future that gives those all around you the inspiration and hope to set their own past on fire.

TRAVEL LIGHT

Experienced travelers are easily recognizable by how little they take with them. The exceptions would be my wife and daughter. They have plenty of traveling experience to know better, but on the same trip across the world where I have found that all I need is a carry-on, they bring so much luggage that one would conclude we were moving, not simply visiting. What's most frustrating to me is not that they choose to bring more luggage than they could possibly need; it's not that they ruin my speedy exit from the airport because we have to wait an hour for their luggage; it's that I know without any doubt that I will be carrying their luggage down every street, through every transition, while they pretend to mind and keep offering to carry their own luggage. As usual, I'll decline. I mean, how would it look if I was strolling with my little carry-on bag, and Kim and Mariah were lugging huge pieces of luggage? The moment I decided to do that, someone across the world would recognize us, take a photograph, put it on Instagram, and show what a lousy husband and father I am. But the truth is, the more you travel, the more you know how little you need.

There have been several occasions over the years when my luggage would shift from a domestic terminal to an international terminal, and I would be required to go through security and back through customs to get to my transferring flight to another country. Sometimes I had to decide, *Do I get my luggage or do I catch my flight?* Honestly, it doesn't even matter what I have in the luggage. There is no question. You leave the baggage behind and you get on the plane. It's more important to get where you are going than to take what you brought with you.

On one particular flight from Los Angeles to London and then transferring to Hong Kong, my luggage decided it was far more interested in visiting Cairo, Egypt.

When I went to pick up my luggage at the London airport to transfer it to the Asian flight, it was nowhere to be found. It wasn't that my luggage was MIA, as the airline knew exactly where it went; it just happened to be in a completely different part of the world from where I was going. But not all was lost. I experienced a wonderful upgrade and had perhaps the best flight of my life. The airline provided a gourmet chef on the plane, scheduled massages, and they gave me a sweat suit to wear, which really came in handy because that was all the extra clothes I had when I got to Hong Kong. I could complain all day about not having my luggage when I arrived in Hong Kong, but the truth is, I did just fine without it.

One thing I have learned after traveling over a million miles across the world is that you can pretty much do without everything you think you must have. After all, it's just your baggage, which is what I have discovered over a lifetime is what most of us keep dragging around everywhere we go. We act as if our things are our treasures, but they are not treasure; they are just baggage.

If for no other reason, it's important to set your past on fire to set yourself free from all the things that you keep holding on to that keep holding on to you. And that doesn't go just for physical possessions. Set the bitterness on fire; light it up with forgiveness and watch it burn. Put the wounds behind you, put the betrayal behind you, put the disappointment behind you, put the regret behind you, put the failures behind you—or better yet, cut them into pieces, turn them into an altar, and let them burn. All that stuff is just baggage. It's too much weight to carry, and it will weigh you down and hold you back.

I was standing in the lobby of a hotel talking to a friend, and although our conversation was interesting, the one happening right next to us was far more interesting. I began listening in on the story of a man named Mark Floyd, who then became a new friend. He does not draw attention to himself. He comes across like he's just an everyday guy. The lack of flash might blind you to the genius that defines this man. And the only thing that might make it harder to see that genius is the raw courage that fuels his brilliant mind.

What caught my attention was his telling the story of when he lost $20 million of his investors' money. You might at first glance consider that a horrific failure. I'm an optimist, so my immediate thought was, *What kind of man gets the opportunity to* *lose $20 million?* It takes great risk and great courage to experience great loss and great failure, so I was intrigued.

Mark had a business idea. He was sure it was a can't-miss idea, and he was so compelling and persuasive that he found investors who believed in both his idea and his ability to execute that idea. They trusted him with their money and he lost it all. What would you do in a situation like that? Me? I might just set myself on fire or play my violin like Nero as I watched Rome burn all around me.

Mark did the unexpected. He went back to those investors and faced them. That, by itself, took an immense amount of integrity and courage. He faced them and told them that he had lost all their money, but he had a way forward. He had a way of setting their past on fire and stepping into a new and better future. This, of course, would require them to give him more money. He had a different idea—a better idea, an idea that couldn't miss. All they would need to do is trust him and his idea, and he would not only return to them all the money that was lost, but they would also reap the benefits of this new endeavor.

I'm not sure what the first idea was. Mark has explained it to me, but I just can't understand it. The second idea, though, I can wrap my head around a little better. The second idea was DSL (digital subscriber line), which has something to do with fiber optics, communication systems, techy stuff. I don't even pretend to fully understand DSL; I just know that the modern world has been revolutionized by it. Not only did those investors regain the millions they lost, but they walked away with unimaginable wealth. I suppose one has to be willing to lose millions to make billions.

Mark is a reminder to me that when you stand in the ashes of failure, you have two choices: you can sit and wallow in your failure and spend your life marked by dust and ashes, or you can get up, dust yourself off, cut the plows to pieces, create an altar, set your past on fire, and create a new future. I am less impressed with the genius of Mark's ideas, although they are impressive indeed, and far more impressed with the courage it took to go back to those who had been burned in his past and refuse to leave them there and instead take them into the future he was certain he was going to create.

A BURN LIST

Sometimes setting your past on fire isn't about facing a particular failure in your life or admitting that your life is a failure. Sometimes it feels as if life has failed you. But what do you do when you look back on your life and realize that an endless number of bad decisions have left you trapped and suffocating in your failure?

Natasha Ray found herself sleeping with her two children in their car, which she parked outside of the apartment complex from which she had just been evicted. Natasha had moved recently from Washington, DC, and was now living in Los Angeles.

Instead of finding the new life she hoped for, she found herself homeless and unemployed with two children to care for. Yet for Natasha, living out of her car and showering in public restrooms was better than the life she had left. Somehow she knew that this was a temporary setback. She had a future to pursue and was determined to let nothing stop her from getting there.

Just months before in DC, she had left an abusive boyfriend who had spent twelve years in prison. Natasha, now thirty-seven years old, had been with him since the age of sixteen. I cannot imagine that she knew at such a young age that she was committing herself to a lifetime of pain and heartbreak. She did everything she could to make that relationship work, for a while driving four hours in each direction with her kids just so they could see their father. She put up with the physical abuse, his infidelity, and his criminal behavior, convincing herself that it was the right thing to do. A strange part of the dynamic of being abused is that one becomes dependent on the abuser, which makes it hard to find the courage to create a better life. It is even more difficult when all the victim has been told is that he or she is nothing and will never be anything.

But a month after her boyfriend was released from prison, Natasha was lying in bed when she heard a voice shouting in her head one simple word: *Go!* She got in her car, pulled together the $2,500 she had managed to save, and with the help of a friend began driving across the country from the nation's capital to the City of Angels. I wonder how many of us would have the courage to literally drive from coast to coast to leave the life we knew to pursue a life we could only hope for.

Frankly, when I came to know Natasha, I never would have guessed that her past was filled with so much pain and brokenness. She's an amazingly optimistic and hopeful person, always ready to encourage and elevate someone's day. Natasha works for a unique men's-grooming franchise known as Hammer & Nails. If you watch *Shark Tank,* you might remember the pitch from salon owner Michael Elliot. Although he did not achieve the funding he hoped for from the show, the public exposure allowed him to find funding to launch his vision for men to never again have to go to a women's salon to have their nails done.

Ironically, for me it was an unexpected comment that led me to walk into Hammer & Nails. I was speaking at an event where a room was filled with high-end businesspeople, most of whom had never considered the possibility of needing Christ or even believing in God. After a brief presentation on why Jesus was worth their consideration, and a wonderfully fiery and dynamic question-and-answer session, a woman came up to me— we'll call her Rita. After expressing how impactful the evening had been, she made a brief comment that completely caught me off guard. She said, "The one thing that surprises me is that a person who pays such careful attention to all of these aspects of life pays so little attention to his nails," and she proceeded to tell me that I should seriously consider taking care of this detail of my appearance.

Honestly, I felt really irritated. I was trying to talk to her about the deeper things of life, about the existence of God, about the importance of Jesus; I was trying to help her find what her soul was desperately searching for, and the only thing she could think about was the fact that my nails were not manicured. I thanked her for her input and left feeling that she had missed the whole point of the evening. By the next day, I had this thought: if my lack of attention to my nails was in any way an obstacle for someone coming to know Jesus, I would rather humble myself and take care of the problem. It just never seemed very masculine to get a manicure, so I cannot express how grateful I was to find a place with such a masculine name as Hammer & Nails.

I met Natasha again because she was my manicurist, and as I listened to her story, I realized she was the reason why I walked through that door. Here was a woman who had spent twenty years of her life in an abusive relationship and had to find a way to raise her two beautiful sons, Santana and Mateo, while leaving a past that would certainly jeopardize all their futures, to pursue the possibility of creating a better life for all of them. Here was a woman who had been homeless and lived out of her car, whose address had been a parking lot in Los Angeles, who had found the job as a manicurist and had then become the general manager of the original Melrose location and now has been made the national director of training for Hammer & Nails. And on top of that, she has created her own organic body-care line called Organic Body Society, and of course her company is the official distributor of body lotions and scrubs to all Hammer & Nails locations.

When Natasha arrived in Los Angeles three years ago, she got a tattoo on her hand that was simply the word *free* inside of a heart. I said to her, "I would love to share your story with the world. You exemplify for me what it means to strike the last arrow, to give everything you have, to leave nothing for the next life, to choose to live without regret and be truly free." But it was more specific than that. I told her that I wanted to place her story in the chapter called "Set Your Past on Fire."

She said, "I have goose bumps. That's the name of your chapter?"

I said, "Yes. Why does that matter so much?"

"Didn't I tell you what I did right before we came to Los Angeles?"

"No. What happened?"

She said that during her trip from DC to Los Angeles, she drove past an Indian reservation. She told me, "Somehow I knew I needed to learn acceptance and find purpose, and to do that I needed to leave the past behind." So while on that Indian reservation, she started a small fire. On wide-ruled notebook paper, she wrote down everyone and everything in her life that had hurt her. She wrote down every pain she had ever felt, every moment of suffering she had ever gone through. She wrote them all down, every last one. And after she had exhausted every painful memory and written them within the borders of those pages, she placed them in the fire. She burned them to let them go. She literally set her past on fire.

Maybe that's what you need to do right now: start a fire and take every memory that continues to wound you, all the pain, all the regret, all the bitterness and disappointment, all the moments of betrayal and every failure and take them out of your heart and put them in the fire. Don't take your past into your future. Don't take it with you. Your past will be your future until you have the courage to create a new future.

When the prophet Jeremiah was at the end of himself, when he felt as if God had let him down, when he accused God of deceit and betrayal, when he was certain God had abandoned him and wanted nothing else to do with him, he found himself at a similar intersection. It's in these moments that we are most at risk to be swallowed up by our pasts and lose our futures. It's in these moments that there seems to be more pain than joy, more suffering than hope, more regret than possibility. We can't always stop and build a fire, but we can live our lives in such a way that that fire always burns within us.

When given the choice to live in the past or to move into God's future, Jeremiah expressed these words:

> If I say, "I will not mention his word
>   or speak anymore in his name,"
> his word is in my heart like a fire,
>   a fire shut up in my bones.

I am weary of holding it in;

indeed, I cannot.[1]

There is a fire that will burn bright on our darkest nights, and it will always give light to the future we long for. But what must fuel that fire is the material from yesterday that would keep us from the future that awaits us. I don't know where you've been or what you've been through, and it could be that for you the past is like an anchor holding you back and pulling you under. So no matter how dark it is, it's time to stop looking back and start looking forward. If you want to find the life that will guide your way, then set your past on fire.

5

REFUSE TO STAY BEHIND

On July 6, 2014, I received an unexpected text from someone I had met only once. Don Williams had one simple question: Was I interested in going to the finals of the World Cup? The text response of this major soccer fan was short and sweet: "Yes!" Then I got on the phone to ascertain whether this was a cruel joke or perhaps some new approach from a "Nigerian prince" scam artist. When I talked to Don, he explained that his brother Doug worked in the global sports market and that through Doug's partnerships with Adidas and FIFA (Féderation Internationale de Football Association), Don had been offered the opportunity to travel with Doug to the World Cup. At the last minute Don was unable to go, and this led him to ask me if I would be interested in taking his place.

If I remember correctly, I had met Don only once and had never met Doug. So I had to ask the question: "Why would you invite me?" After all, they lived on the East Coast; I live on the

West Coast. Surely they had an endless number of friends who would jump on this opportunity.

Don said they were wondering, "Who do we know that would rearrange their life with a moment's notice and say yes to getting on a plane, flying to Rio de Janeiro, and attending the World Cup final?" And he continued, "That's when your name came up. We all agreed that Erwin McManus would."

I have to admit, I loved being the name that popped up when they wondered who would move heaven and earth to make this kind of adventure possible.

When I said yes, yes didn't even seem possible. I said yes on the sixth of the month and would have to fly out by the tenth to make it to the finals on the thirteenth. I didn't have a plane ticket; I didn't have a place to stay; I didn't have a visa. I didn't have anything that I would need to make this trip work.

But I love soccer. I had never been to Brazil, which is the mecca of soccer, and I couldn't imagine a more epic adventure than to fly to Rio de Janeiro, with just a few days' notice, to watch the greatest sport in the world in its greatest context.

I don't know if Aaron, who turned twenty-five the same week I was headed to Rio, will ever let me live down the moment when I told him, "Happy birthday, Son. I am leaving tomorrow for the World Cup. I'm sorry I can't take you with me, but there's only one ticket available." Yet having been raised in the midst of a life filled with adventure and spontaneity,

Aaron more than understood that this was an opportunity of a lifetime.

My wife, Kim, didn't even blink an eye. She knew that if it was at all possible, I needed to make it happen.

I immediately called someone on my staff for help. I said, "Holly, get me a ticket to Rio de Janeiro. I'm going to the World Cup." That was so much easier said than done. We needed to get not only from LA to Rio but also from Rio to DC. At the same time, Holly began looking for hotels where I could stay while in Rio. I remember her telling me that she could get me into Rio but that there wasn't a single hotel room in the entire city available. So if I went to the World Cup, I would not have a place to stay. Was I sure I still wanted to book the flight?

I said, "Yes, just get me there. I can find a lobby somewhere to sleep and shower. I'll find a way of working it out when I get there." After all, didn't Jesus say that when we travel, we should take nothing with us?

And then there was the problem with the visa. When Holly contacted the Brazilian embassy, she was told that it can take several weeks to acquire a visa for entry into their country. So we thought that we should hire professionals to solve the problem. We found a company that accelerates the visa process for a living, and they had no more success than we did. Even an expedited process would be weeks, not days. This obstacle seemed insurmountable, and it would have been easy to decide it just wasn't meant to be. But sometimes we have to refuse to stay behind.

I contacted Don's brother Doug, and we proceeded to contact FIFA in Germany to see if they could help me get into Brazil. After all, this was life or death! FIFA graciously invited me to be a part of their department of marketing for one day so that I could secure an expedited visa to the World Cup.

I personally went to the Brazilian embassy on Thursday, knowing my flight was leaving on Friday. I explained to them my desperate situation and how I needed to leave for Rio in the next twenty-four hours. I gave them my official letter of invitation from FIFA, and after several glances at my documents and a deep stare into my soul, the woman processing my passport asked me what time my flight was the next day. I think it was around two in the afternoon. So she told me to come back the next day by noon and my visa would be waiting for me. The next day, I literally went from my house to the Brazilian embassy, grabbed my visa, rushed to the airport, and boarded a flight to Rio de Janeiro to go to the World Cup. Did I mention I had no place to stay?

While at the airport, I had a thought that I should post on Instagram and Twitter that I was on my way to the World Cup in Rio de Janeiro. I should also casually mention I had no place to stay. Maybe someone in the virtual world would find solutions for me. And that's exactly what happened. It's amazing how powerful the words "On my way to Rio for the finals of the World Cup, have no place to stay" can be. Only minutes had passed, when a newly married couple in Rio responded, "We will pick you up at the airport and you can stay with our family. We'd love to have you."

How could I have known that a beautiful Brazilian couple who had actually been married at Mosaic was back in Rio visiting their family at the same time I would be arriving? Where they were staying was outside of Rio, a block from the ocean. Their family was as gracious and hospitable as anyone could ever hope for. They did have one request: Could I stay and have breakfast with their family? They would be very interested to have a conversation about God.

Breakfast must have lasted hours. It was perhaps the best part of my journey to the World Cup finals. We talked about life and family, about God and spirituality. Our most poignant conversations were about who Jesus was and what it meant for him to be the Savior of the world, which is a fascinating conversation in the city renowned across the world for its giant statue of Jesus standing over the city.

I stayed with the family one night and then received a text from the man who had invited me to the World Cup, letting me know that he had changed rooms so that he could accommodate my staying with him. He explained that coming into the city during the finals would be almost impossible and that this way I would be in the heart of the city and access would be simplified. I was amazed how all of this had come together in just a matter of days and how now I would be staying in the heart of the city during one of the most extraordinary celebrations in the world.

I walked the streets of Rio de Janeiro virtually all night against all the advice I had been given. Thousands upon thousands of people danced in the streets, sang their nations' victory songs, and celebrated before the game as if their teams had already been found victorious. And there I was on July 13, 2014, watching Germany and Argentina compete for the World Cup. If I'd had a bucket list, this definitely would have been near the top. I could not believe that I was in Rio de Janeiro, Brazil, at the finals of the World Cup and that a week before I'd had no idea this was even a possibility. I could not help but think of how many times in life we are invited into an extraordinary adventure and into opportunities that exist only in our imaginations and we let them slip away.

DEFINING DECISIONS

All of us have life principles—whether stated or unstated, conscious or unconscious—that define us. Although we might never give them language, we always give them power. You will know yours if you pay attention to the patterns in your life. For example, I know a lot of people who have a recurring theme in their life of *I wish I had done that*. Others have a recurring theme of *If I could choose differently, I would*. Still others have a recurring theme of *How come that never happens for me?*

If you notice that you're constantly in a state of regret, it may be that you need a seismic shift in your guiding life principles. Here is one that I assure you will change your life forever: *Refuse to stay behind*. Never ever opt out of the opportunities that move you in the direction of your dreams, your purpose, your passions.

Decide ahead of time; do not allow yourself to be paralyzed in the moment with indecision; know what you are about; know what your life is given to; know what matters to you and always move forward in that direction.

People who are constantly praying about everything may be doing too much talking and not enough listening. The point of prayer is response. And once God has spoken, you don't need to pray about that anymore—unless, of course, you are trying to change his mind. There are things I don't need to pray about anymore. I already prayed about them. I know the answer. What I don't need is clarity. What I do need is courage and conviction. I have been married for more than thirty years. I don't need to pray for a wife. I don't need to pray about whether I should love her; I don't need to pray about whether I should be faithful; I don't even need to pray about whether I should be a good husband. I already have the answers to all of this. If you think about it, there are so many things you don't need to pray about. *Should I kill him?* Don't need to pray about it. *Should I steal that?* Don't need to pray about that. *Should I be a Lakers fan?* I don't need to pray about that.

A few years ago, staff members from an extraordinary church in the Midwest contacted me about leaving Los Angeles and moving to serve with them. I was able to answer immediately: thanks but no thanks. They encouraged me to take some time to pray about it. I told them I didn't need to since I had already prayed about it. Thirty years ago, I prayed about coming to LA. I committed my life to Mosaic more than twenty years ago. The wonderful thing about having clear yeses in your life is that they allow you to have clear nos as well. I don't need to pray about whether I should exercise, stay healthy, or eat well. I may need to pray for the strength to do all of that, but I am pretty clear about what I should do.

Frankly, over the years, many young men have come and asked me how they can have my life, but what quickly becomes clear is that they want the life without the path. They want my life without my wounds; they want my life without my scars. In fact, they don't actually want my life; they want the rewards. I am the first to admit that I live an enviable life. I love my life. My life is full of adventure and surprise. It has also been full of suffering and hardship. And while it may seem to you a meaningless thing to get to be at the finals of the World Cup, I can tell you that the same mind-set that got me there allowed me to walk the streets of Damascus, Syria, and of Phnom Penh, Cambodia, and of Islamabad, Pakistan, and many other streets I was told not to walk. I am absolutely convinced that the world has opened its doors to me because I opened my heart to the world. I know without any doubt that I never would have seen one exotic place in the world had I not given my life to the unromantic and easily overlooked communities of the urban poor, where I served for more than a decade of my life.

When people come to Mosaic on the corner of Hollywood Boulevard and La Brea Avenue, they see thousands of painfully attractive people who represent the most talented and gifted people in the world. But what they often miss is the fact that our community was born out of a heart shaped by working for years with the homeless, the indigent, prostitutes, drug dealers, and urban poor. I do not see these as different lives. What I am certain of is that the same guiding principle has led me throughout my whole life. The same guiding principle that put me in the middle of drug cartels also put me in a stadium in Rio de Janeiro. I'm not going to watch life happen. I refuse to be the audience. Life is not meant for observation. Life is cruel in this: if you are willing to be left behind, the future will leave you in the past and opportunity will depart.

I cannot say it enough: if you are going to live a life that never settles, if you are going to live the life that God created you to live, if you are going to be able to look back on your life and know you have lived it without cause for regret, then refuse to stay behind. No one can make this shift for you. No one can create this change on your behalf. You have to stop waiting for someone to call you off the bench and put you in the game. You need to get up and refuse to remain on the sidelines any longer. You need to get to the front of the battle. You need to stop letting life slip through your fingers and grab hold of it and refuse to let go.

LOOKING FOR VOLUNTEERS

The athletes and other students at the University of Tennessee are called the Volunteers. I've always loved that name, the symbolism behind it. There's something powerful about a person who doesn't have to be drafted—something more noble about warriors who stand on the front line not out of obligation but because they volunteered to risk their lives for the freedom of others. If no one chooses you, volunteer.

This was a driving characteristic in the life of Elisha. We saw in an earlier chapter that Elisha was out plowing the fields when Elijah walked by and placed his mantle on Elisha, symbolizing that he was going to be transferring his prophetic status to the younger man. A later event proved that Elisha was eager and assertive in receiving that new status, that new role: he volunteered.

In the book of 2 Kings, we are told that Elijah is about to be taken up to heaven in a whirlwind and that Elijah and Elisha are on their way to Gilgal.[1]

Elijah says to Elisha, "Stay here; the LORD has sent me to Bethel."

Elisha replies, "As surely as the LORD lives and as you live, I will not leave you."

So they go down to Bethel together.

At Bethel a large company of prophets come out to Elisha and ask him, "Do you know that the LORD is going to take your master from you today?"

"Yes, I know," Elisha replies. "So be quiet."

Then Elijah says to him, "Stay here, Elisha; the LORD has sent me to Jericho."

Still determined to stick with Elijah, Elisha says, "As surely as the LORD lives and as you live, I will not leave you."

So they go to Jericho.

The company of prophets at Jericho goes to Elisha and asks him, "Do you know that the LORD is going to take your master from you today?"

Elisha again responds, "Yes, I know. So be quiet." (You're seeing the pattern developing here.)

Then Elijah says to him, "Stay here; the LORD has sent me to the Jordan."

And Elisha replies a third time, "As surely as the LORD lives and as you live, I will not leave you."

So the two of them walk on.

The story goes on to tell us that fifty men from the company of the prophets stand at a distance facing the place where Elijah and Elisha have stopped at the Jordan. Elijah takes his cloak, rolls it up, and strikes the water with it. The water divides to the right and to the left, and the two of them cross over on dry ground.

When they have crossed, Elijah says to Elisha, "Tell me, what can I do for you before I am taken from you?"

Then Elisha asks—

Wait! Before we get to Elisha's request, it's important to note that in each stop along the way, Elisha is not the only prophet who has an opportunity to keep traveling with Elijah. All other prophets choose to stay where they are rather than travel ahead with Elijah. They know he is going to the end of his journey, but they

are comfortable with remaining behind. It is only Elisha who refuses to be left behind.

It is not coincidental that Elijah repeatedly gives Elisha the
opportunity to stay behind. He even commands him (or at the
very least implores him), "Stay here." No one would think any less
of Elisha if he stopped at Bethel, remained in Jericho, or never left
the safety of Gilgal. It is only when Elijah and Elisha stand alone
on the other side of the Jordan that Elijah finally asks him the
question, "What can I do for you?"

Then Elisha asks the most incredible of all things: "Let me
inherit a double portion of your spirit."

Here's where sometimes life gets a little tricky. There is no
small number of people who are willing to ask for a double portion of what someone else has been given; it's just that they want
to ask for this at Gilgal or Bethel or Jericho. They want God to do
in them and for them far more than what's reasonable based on
where they have allowed God to take them. I am convinced that
we don't get a double portion of God's Spirit by watching Elijah walk away while standing at Jericho. When we choose to remain behind, we also leave behind all that God desires to do in us
and for us and through us. If we want to inherit a double portion
of the spirit of Elijah, we need to walk in the steps of Elijah until
he leaves no more footprints.

Elijah responds to Elisha, "You have asked a difficult thing, . . .
yet if you see me when I am taken from you, it will be yours—
otherwise, it will not."

We are then brought into what may be the most dramatic exit from the human story found anywhere in history. Here it is verbatim:

> As they were walking along and talking together, suddenly a chariot of fire and horses of fire appeared and separated the two of them, and Elijah went up to heaven in a whirlwind. Elisha saw this and cried out, "My father! My father! The chariots and horsemen of Israel!" And Elisha saw him no more. Then he took hold of his garment and tore it in two.
>
> Elisha then picked up Elijah's cloak that had fallen from him and went back and stood on the bank of the Jordan. He took the cloak that had fallen from Elijah and struck the water with it. "Where now is the LORD, the God of Elijah?" he asked. When he struck the water, it divided to the right and to the left, and he crossed over.
>
> The company of the prophets from Jericho, who were watching, said, "The spirit of Elijah is resting on Elisha." And they went to meet him and bowed to the ground before him.[2]

This story is about more than what Elisha experienced; it is about who Elisha was as a person. We all want chariots of fire without going beyond the point of no return. Elisha understood what it meant to live a life that holds nothing back and leaves nothing undone. Elisha was given multiple opportunities to opt out. For him, this was a choice he had made long before. Elisha is the man who cut his plow into pieces and slaughtered his oxen and gave them as an offering to God and a gift to his people. For Elisha, there was never an option of turning back and there was never an option of staying behind.

When you understand this man, you will understand his anger when the king stops striking the arrow long before victory has been secured. When God tells you to strike an arrow, you just keep striking and striking and striking and you do not stop until you hear heaven shout, "It is finished."[3]

BORN TO RUN

When our kids, Aaron and Mariah, were about seven and four years old, I decided to take them to El Salvador to meet my grandparents, see the home I grew up in, and experience the country of my birth. Kim was not able to travel with us, so it was just me and the kids. It was my first effort to take both kids on an international trip, but I was hopeful it would all work out well.

We never even made it onto the flight together. The kids and I said our good-byes to Kim, went through security, and were preparing to board the flight to San Salvador, when Mariah lost her mind. She began screaming and crying, "I want my mommy! I want my mommy! I don't want to go. I don't want to go."

Now, you have to understand the context. I look Spanish; my children look Swedish. Both Aaron and Mariah were blond, and Mariah, especially with her green eyes, looked like she was someone else's child. When Mariah began crying frantically for her mother, it looked as though I was kidnapping somebody else's child. Nothing I could do would calm her, and finally I realized this wasn't going to work and we began running down the terminal back to the security entrance, hoping to catch Kim before she headed home.

Fortunately, we were able to make the awkward transfer of giving my daughter back to her mother, and then it became a guy trip. For the next several years, I would always alternate opportunities to travel with me between Aaron and Mariah. I didn't want to be preferential, and I wanted to give them both an opportunity to travel the world and have wonderful adventures with their dad. Mariah, being younger and having had a bad first experience, became afraid to travel. So every time it was her turn, she would decline and Aaron would get to go in her place. Aaron began racking up countries all over the world. He traveled to more than thirty countries before he was eighteen.

Mariah, for the first few years, stayed at home and would hear about our adventures. And then one day it hit her: *What am I doing? I am giving up my adventures to my brother because I'm afraid to fly.* It was to my wonderful surprise one day when I offered her a chance to go with me somewhere across the world and she said yes. You cannot imagine the disappointment on Aaron's face. He had become accustomed to getting both his turn and her turn. But something had clicked inside Mariah. She realized the incredible opportunities she was missing. It was as if it happened in a moment. It was as if she decided, *I refuse to stay behind.*

That was just the beginning. Now she is not even twenty-four and has already caught up with how many countries Aaron has been to. Not only has she traveled to nearly forty countries around the world, but she has journeyed without us to some of the most dangerous places on the planet as well. If anyone has received a double portion of our spirit, it's this little girl who decided to choose differently.

While my family has had the great privilege of traveling across the world, I am reminded that Jesus never walked far from the place of his birth. This great adventure that God calls us on does not require jet setting across the planet. Sometimes our greatest quests are within walking distance of our front doors. Sometimes the great challenge God has placed in front of us comes in the most unexpected situations, such as being good husbands, good wives, good parents.

Sometimes your geography doesn't change at all but the journey is still long and hard. Becoming the man your family deserves is no small endeavor. Having the courage to live a life of honor and integrity may be the greatest battle you will ever face. Leaving the job you have for the career you long for can feel no different than traveling to a distant land you have never known. The starting point for all of us is to look at your life and ask, *Am I still on the journey forward, or have I found myself settling when I should have been advancing?*

And this is one of the ways I know all of us can change. Maybe you've spent your life opting out. Maybe you've unconsciously made it a life principle to settle for less. I've discovered God to be incredibly gracious. Like Elijah offering Elisha the opportunity to stay behind, God does not force us into the more. Sometimes he doesn't even invite us; he merely asks, "Whom shall I send? Who will go for us?" And he waits to hear what voice will emerge out of the crowd. "Here am I. I'll go!"[4]

Don't wait to be asked—volunteer. Volunteer to go forward. Volunteer to go further. Volunteer to go harder. You cannot pioneer out of obligation. It is not an adventure if it is not your choice. You have to want it. You have to want more. If you are going to be greedy, this is the right place to be greedy. Want everything God has for you. Want more than others think you can obtain. Why settle for a single portion if a double portion can be yours for the asking?

I do think it's important to note that Elisha's receiving a double portion of the spirit of Elijah never translated into double the wealth or double the fame. This is important in that often we want God to give us more of the wrong things while settling for less of the things that matter most. Elisha received a double portion of the power of God's Spirit. I cannot even begin to understand the full implications of that. I just know that I want a double portion of that double portion.

So these questions need to be asked: If you are not where you want to be, why do you keep choosing to stay where you are? If you know there is a future waiting for you, why do you choose to stay trapped in the past? What will it take to jar you out of the security of where you are to pursue what can be obtained only in an uncertain future?

More often than not, the journey to where God wants to take us requires that we travel further than we ever expected. Like the early pioneers who began in New York and Boston determined to make it to San Francisco but instead chose to settle in Oklahoma and Missouri, we may have become settlers far too soon. Now, if you are supposed to be in Oklahoma or Missouri, that's a good thing. But if you simply gave up because the journey was longer and harder than you expected, then you have become a settler when you should still be a pioneer. The unfortunate reality is that many of us would choose our comfort rather than our destiny, would choose safety over opportunity, would rather settle for less than sacrifice more.

Elisha refused to stay behind even when doing so would have been so much more convenient and even more reasonable than continuing forward. And his risk did not come with any guarantees or any promises. Elijah offered him nothing that would entice him to continue his journey with him. In fact, the opposite was true. Elijah kept insisting that Elisha stay behind with the rest and allow Elijah to continue his journey alone. But for Elisha this question had already been answered. He didn't leave everything he knew and everything he had to end his journey before it had even begun; he was going to see it through regardless of the cost or consequence.

THE MOMENTUM OF ACTION

I have always traveled a lot, but lately my wife has been giving me a run for my money. In the last few months, Kim has been in India, Indonesia, Bangladesh, Vietnam, Argentina, and China. It may seem strange, but we rarely travel together. She did insist, however, that I join her on her most recent trip. She was traveling to the borders of Lebanon and Syria to dive headfirst into the Syrian refugee crisis that has quickly become perhaps the greatest humanitarian crisis of our time, with more than eleven million Syrians who have been displaced from their homes and over five million who have had to flee their own country. Though the numbers keep changing, what we know is that millions of innocent people have been displaced as a result of a vicious civil war.

But to call it a civil war is an understatement. The conflict is far more than a local fight for territory. This conflict has entangled the world from the United States and Europe to Russia. It seems the world is at war within the borders of Syria. The conflict is complex and both deeply political and profoundly religious. On one level it is the conflict between the Shia and Sunni Muslims. And frankly, as much as we try to make it black and white, we need scorecards to know who the good guys and bad guys are.

This wasn't our first trip to Syria. Just two weeks before the 9/11 disaster, not only Kim and I but also our kids were in Beirut and the Bekáa Valley. Back then, the great concern for many of the Lebanese were the Shiite Muslims. From a Western perspective, the Shiites were personified by Iran and the Ayatollah Khomeini. I rarely heard anything back then about the Sunnis. It was just a couple years before that when I walked the streets of Damascus. And although I was told that Damascus was an epicenter for global terrorism, I found the Syrian people to be incredibly inviting and hospitable to me. I never once felt in danger. But while in Lebanon, I could see and feel the oncoming violence and instability of the region. We would drive and see Lebanese tanks and soldiers patrolling a region and within minutes see Syrian tanks and soldiers patrolling an adjoining region. It felt like a game of checkers, with two nations and two armies fighting for the same square.

But everything was different on our 2016 trip. There was no Syrian occupation in Lebanon. This time it was a different Syrian occupation. This time it wasn't an influx of soldiers with weapons but rather two million refugees who barely had the shirts on their backs and who came not with weapons in their hands but empty handed.

The events of 9/11 introduced us to al-Qaeda, which left our concerns about Hezbollah in the past, as we were now facing a new danger. And al-Qaeda has seemed almost like a bad dream since the emergence of a new danger known as ISIS. And here's where things get tricky. ISIS is a terrorist cell that is an extreme and violent expression of Sunni Islam, which in a black-and-white world makes it clear that the Sunnis are the enemy, which only exacerbates the dilemma for the two million refugees who find themselves homeless, starving, and desperate. These two million refugees, we discovered, are also Sunni Muslims. Their businesses were destroyed, their homes annihilated, their fathers and sons murdered, their nation lost to them. Bashar al-Assad, who is a Shiite, has orchestrated a national massacre of the Islamic sect that threatens his rule and opposes his leadership. So now we have Muslims killing Muslims. Or to put it in a different context (say, Belfast not too many years ago), it would be like Catholics and Protestants killing each other, when to the rest of the world it seems they should be brothers and allies.

The Syrian refugee crisis is relatively new, and as bad as it is, it's going to get worse. Lebanon is a small country with a population of only four million. Can you imagine the complexities of a nation with four million people trying to absorb more than two million refugees? That would be the equivalent of roughly one hundred sixty million refugees crossing the US borders. The population of Texas is around twenty-seven million. That means that more than five times the population of Texas would have entered our country overnight with nowhere to live, no food or water, and nowhere to go. And just to make it a little more difficult, interwoven into two million innocent people would be a small number of the most violent and vicious religious and political extremists the world has ever known. What you know is that 99.9 percent of the people are innocent; what you cannot know is who is included in the 0.1 percent that has come to destroy you and your freedom.

So there we were, sitting thirty minutes away from the battle lines with ISIS, listening to the stories of heartbroken refugees who had lost not only all their worldly possessions but their dignity as well. The Lebanese government has been furiously at work to walk the fine line between hospitality and security. Lebanon is a land of immigrants and refugees. More than half a million Palestinians live as permanent refugees within the borders of Lebanon. Now the Lebanese people have opened up their arms to these two million refugees that most of the world will not welcome. At the same time, they do not wish to be the permanent solution to this humanitarian crisis, so all the settlements are temporary. Even the refugees' designation expresses the Lebanese people's concern. They are called *interim tent settlements*—ITS. There is purposely no access to running water, electricity, or utilities of any kind. After all, the settlements are intended to be temporary. They are *interim* settlements. Yet many of the families have already been there four or five years.

As I listened to the stories, I was struck over and over again by the recurring theme of all they left behind. These were not people who were poor or indigent in their previous lives; these were craftsmen and tradesmen, professionals and business owners. They had homes and families and a future. The war cost them everything. They watched their businesses destroyed, their homes bombed, and their loved ones murdered. Yet when we asked them what they missed most, they never spoke of their work or their possessions or even the homes they left behind. They always talked about the family and friends who did not come with them.

But what struck me the most was the lack of regret that their present circumstances seemed to create. I thought that knowing now what they had fled to would surely change their perspective on their choice to flee their home and their country. Certainly their bleak and hopeless circumstances would make them wish they had never left in the first place. Yet, across the board, I found the same perspective to be true: They would have done it again without hesitation. If they could change anything, they would simply make sure no one was left behind.

I met a woman who lost her husband to the war, whose son was kidnapped, whose relatives were murdered, and who now found herself alone taking care of her three grandchildren, all under ten years of age. She could see no way forward and became destitute and desperate. I heard her describe the forty-day trek leaving her home in Syria in pursuit of safety in the Bekáa Valley. Forty days through war and violence, across mountains and amid grueling conditions. Yet not once did she regret her decision, even though it had cost her everything.

I met a family whose oldest son, around ten years old, had stopped speaking as a result of the trauma of watching his father dragged out of his house and taken as a prisoner. Others will forever be traumatized by having watched their loved ones killed before their eyes.

One moment I will never forget is when we entered the tent of a still-intact family. The father invited us in and sat with us as we listened to his story and met his wife and children sitting in a tent he had made over a period of two weeks built on a property filled with dirt and mud. Yet when we walked inside, it was meticulously clean. It was easy to sense the pride they had and their determination to make the best of a horrible situation. He offered us tea when there were about ten of us in the tent sitting together. Each of us graciously declined, not wanting to use up their resources. I'll never forget how, moments later, their children brought tea for all of us anyway. If that wasn't surprising enough, I watched the father pour the first two cups of tea and for some undisclosed reason decide they did not meet his standard. He sent them back and the children started the process again. Once the tea met the standards necessary for him to share it with his guests, he poured enough for all of us and we graciously accepted.

I was honored to share tea with a man and his family who refused to stay behind, who left everything and risked everything to pursue a life they could never know if they had stayed where they were. I will never forget the beautiful people I met in the Bekáa Valley. Their effect on my life is permanent, indelibly etched in my soul. When I hear the designation Sunni Muslim, it will no longer conjure for me a generalized perception of a people to be feared or despised. I will remember two little girls whose brown eyes melted my heart and who smiled with such uncontrollable happiness that no one would ever know they are victims of unspeakable inhumanity.

CONDUITS OF THE FUTURE

I haven't been able to sleep since I've returned. I've struggled with nightmares. Every time I close my eyes to fall asleep, I'm overwhelmed with unbearable sadness. Over and over again, I have found myself needing all my strength to not start weeping uncontrollably. And all I did was visit. I can't even begin to imagine how those who have to live in that reality have been wounded in the depths of their souls. Yet I know I was exactly where I was supposed to be.

Sometimes God needs us to go somewhere so that we can take others there as well. When we choose to stay behind, the future moves on without us. When we refuse to stay behind, we become conduits to the future.

The irony for me, though, is that I didn't want to go. This trip was not on my schedule; it was on my wife's schedule. It wasn't on my heart; it was on her heart. She began asking me to go six months before, and my response was "Absolutely not. That's your trip, not mine." She kept asking me to say yes and I kept saying no. But my wife is nothing if not tenacious, and she refused to take no as an answer.

Days before we left for Lebanon, she asked me if I was excited about going.

I said, "No. I'm going out of obligation. I'm going because you're making me go. I am going because I want to be happily married. I am going because you'd make me miserable if I didn't go with you."

This was one of those moments when I would have missed what God was trying to do both in me and through me if I'd had my way. It wasn't that I didn't care about the Syrian refugee crisis. It wasn't that I didn't consider the trip important. It's that I had other work to do. I had other priorities. After all, I needed to write this chapter. It's odd that in some strangely distorted way, I convinced myself that I needed to stay behind so that I could tell you to refuse to stay behind. Which is why all of us need people in our lives who refuse to leave us behind, who pull us into the future, who call us into the more. Sometimes it's a war that forces us to leave what we know to pursue a future full of uncertainty. Sometimes God allows us to go through tremendous disruption so that we might choose the path to freedom. At other times God simply uses an invitation and we have to choose our own disruption. We have to decide that we will not stay where we are and lose where we must be.

Perhaps the reason so few of us have received a double portion of God's Spirit is that the lives we have chosen require so little of God because they require so little of us. I do not want to watch God work from a distance. Neither do I want to hear the amazing stories of God's activity in the world as if they are fables made for other people in an ancient time. I want to live the kind of life that cannot be lived without the fullness of Christ in my life.

It may sound greedy, but you need to want seconds. When it comes to God, you need to be Oliver Twist, saying, "Please, sir, I want some more." If God will give Elisha a double portion of Elijah's spirit, then why not you? God is looking for the person who says to him, "I want double of that, and I will travel as far as required. If to go there means to walk alone, then so be it. I refuse to live a life that has already been lived, to be a story already told. Somewhere in my future there will be my chariots of fire."

Refuse to believe that God is less today than he was yesterday. Let whatever lies ahead come, and whatever it costs you, whatever it demands of you, refuse to stay behind.

6

ACT LIKE YOUR LIFE
DEPENDS ON IT

I t's a strange feeling when someone calls you and tells you she wants a key-man policy on your life just in case you suddenly and unexpectedly drop dead before you're supposed to. I was the CEO and creative force behind our multimillion-dollar company, and my business partner and primary investor had been counseled by her attorneys to protect her investment by having me get a life insurance policy that would protect the company in case of my unexpected demise. It's always nice to know that you have value, but it's unnerving when you realize that you may be more valuable dead than alive. It seemed as if it would be a routine procedure to be insured so that the company was protected, and of course I was more than happy to do this, but first it required a full physical and medical clearance to ascertain that I was insurable.

Honestly, I thought this was a no-brainer. I'm a huge propo-nent of living a healthy life. I don't drink. I don't smoke. I don't use any kind of illegal substances. In fact, I almost don't use any legal substances. I avoid even the most common kinds of medical aids. I try never to use pain relievers or aspirin. I try to eat well, exercise often, and stay young for as long as I can. I'm one of those people who believe that physical well-being is a part of one's spiritual stewardship.

So you can only imagine my surprise when my results came back and I was told that I was uninsurable. It was this tricky PSA (prostate-specific antigen) level that threw up a red flag. I had never heard of a PSA level. All I knew about PSAs was that they were public service announcements, and now some obscure medical assessment was telling me that I was too high of a risk to provide life insurance for. I knew the findings were wrong, so I did the test again, and it only confirmed the earlier findings. PSA levels, I was told, are an indication of cancer, so of course this raised great concern for me, my family, and my business partner. Meanwhile, the lab results required me to go through some further tests in which there was poking and prodding, which I do not care to describe in detail. It was a huge relief that they couldn't find anything wrong. As far as they could tell, I was a picture of health.

I waited a couple years and had the doctor redo my blood work and check my PSA levels, which I was convinced would now indicate what I already knew to be true: there was nothing wrong with me. I was perfectly healthy. Unfortunately, the test did not cooperate. My PSA levels came in even higher. At first it did add to my moderate level of concern when my friends who'd had similar circumstances found they were in fact facing real physical danger. I am certainly grateful that PSA testing has helped people in the past catch the warning signs of cancer early enough to save their lives and offer better futures. For me, though, my results were at first only an organizational frustration. I didn't qualify for life insurance, so I couldn't protect my company in case I died, which, of course, is what stood out to me. It wasn't really life insurance; it was death insurance. There is no such thing as life insurance. No one can ensure that someone stays alive. So I lived my life without death insurance.

But I have come to realize that I am responsible for my life insurance. I cannot ensure how long I live, but I can determine that I will live fully while I'm alive. I think this is one of our greatest challenges: that we are so gripped with the fear of death that we become afraid to live. The truth is, my PSA level wasn't telling me anything I didn't already know. It is in my genetic code that I am going to die. No one has to do the blood work. I can save the doctors the trouble and save myself the expense. My life is coming to an end. I'm just not sure how fast the grains of sand are dropping through the hourglass. But I know which way gravity is pulling them. I guess I should be thankful that God gave me the PSA results as a reminder of my terminal condition as a resident on this planet.

So let me just tell you before you hear it from someone else: I'm dying. But so are you. And this really shouldn't be sobering or depressing. It should actually be enlightening and empowering. Because the greatest mistake we make in life is to try to control the things we have no control over and to relinquish control over the things we can affect and change. Wouldn't it be ironic if, instead of sending us through a series of procedures to see if we are at risk of dying, life insurance was determined after a battery of tests checking to see whether we are actually alive?

PROOF OF LIFE

When Jesus's disciples went to the tomb to look for his body, the angel who met them there asked, "Why do you look for the living among the dead?"[1] This is such a telling question. We seem so confused about life and death and even more so about the ambivalent state of being that might be best described as *existence*.

This became more than clear when Kim and I were in Beirut preparing to go into the Bekáa Valley. We were minutes from the border where ISIS was at war with the people of Lebanon. But before we were allowed to jump into our cars, we were asked to take a moment to fill out a series of forms. As I looked over the forms, there was one that jumped right to the surface. Its heading was simply "Proof of Life." I have been to a lot of crazy places in the world, but I have never had to fill out a form demanding proof of life.

There were a series of blank spaces where I could write down questions that could be asked if I were taken hostage, questions that only I and the people closest to me would know the answers to. I knew I should be taking this seriously, but I kept thinking to myself, *What are the proofs of my life?* I wanted to write such things as "He loves dancing in the rain" and "He stops on the side of the road to smell wildflowers and run through fields." The greatest proof of life is when my kids hold me tight and tell me they love me after all these years. I know that's not what the officials in Beirut were looking for. They wanted mundane pieces of information that were confidential enough not to be discoverable by those who might take me hostage. But really, are the facts a proof of *life*, or are they proof of *existence*?

In that moment, for me the real proof of life was that my wife and I, along with an amazing young cinematographer named Jake Viramontez, were willing to enter a part of the world where our lives would be at risk in order to give others a chance for life. In contrast, what is it about us that persuades us to choose mere existence over life? Why is it that we would rather exist for as long as we can rather than to live fully for a short time?

As we were filling out our forms, we were given one caution: "Make sure you put answers to questions that you'll remember. We've had people who filled these out who couldn't even remember their own answers and whose loved ones did not know the answers as well."

If you were to ask the people closest to you, "What would you say are the three most powerful proofs of my life?" what would their answers be? What is your proof of life? What are you doing right now that proves to the world, or at least to those in your world, that you are fully alive?

I have found that life can be incredibly elusive because it exists just on the other side of existence. Most of us are not choosing between life and death; we are choosing between existence and death. We actually never choose to live. We are so afraid of death and all its relatives, such as failure and disappointment and injury, that we actually never choose to live. For all of us, death comes too soon. It comes long before we've taken our final breaths. It's only when we realize we are terminal that we start treating time with the respect it deserves.

NOTHING TO LOSE

I was in Lima, Peru, having been invited to speak at a series of events. Everything about Lima surprised me. I had no idea how beautiful it was. I never could have foreseen that in Lima I would discover some of the best food in the world and some of the most gracious people I had ever encountered. It would have been enough to have found world-class cafés and Paris-trained gourmet chefs to have created memories for a lifetime, but what really stood out to me was the night I was invited to speak at what was once a bullfighting arena. It was my understanding that this was the largest venue in all of Peru. There was a time when thousands of people filled the arena to watch the bullfight-ers take on the noble beasts. I understand the controversy that has been rightfully raised around the cruelty of bullfighting, yet there was a sense that we had stepped into an ancient time, into a different world.

As we were entering the arena where I would speak, our hosts pointed out a spot where the bullfighters would wait before they would face the bulls. As our hosts were proudly walking me through the details of their cultural past, I noticed one particular place and asked them, "What happened over here?"

My guide said, "That corner right there, that's where the bullfighters would go and kneel and pray before they risked their lives in battle."

I asked him if the pastors who speak there ever go to that corner and pray as well, and he said, "No, I don't think that's ever happened."

I said, "Well, if that's where the bullfighters went to find their courage, let's go kneel there and pray ourselves before we enter this battle."

I must confess it was surreal to kneel in the same spot where ancient matadors would pray to God for courage and strength as they entered the battle, but I was now kneeling and praying as I entered the room to speak to fifteen thousand people about who Jesus is and how he has come to give us life. I mean, I'll admit that I have a morbid sense of the finality of life, but I promise you that it works to my advantage. Even though I got to kneel only once where the matadors stopped to pray before they risked their lives, it didn't take a high PSA level or filling out a form titled "Proof of

Life" to cause me to understand the value of life itself. Too many of us act as if we're going to live forever or that life can wait until we're ready to live it. But when it comes to life, we get no trial runs. We get no practice games. And when it comes to life, you need to act as though your life depends on it.

WAITING FOR DAYLIGHT

There is this odd parenthetical story in the middle of the account of Elijah that accentuates the dilemma of life and death. It goes to show that life and death are not sequential; they are concurrent. If you see death as only in your future, you may actually be postponing life into your future as well. Sometimes it takes a desperate condition to make us desperate enough to choose life.

Four men with leprosy sat at the entrance of the city gate. They said to each other, "Why stay here until we die? If we say, 'We'll go into the city'—the famine is there, and we will die. And if we stay here, we will die. So let's go over to the camp of the Arameans and surrender. If they spare us, we live; if they kill us, then we die."[2] I just love the optimism of this observation.

It would be bad enough to be a leper. It would be worse to be a leper in a time of famine. And if it were not bad enough to be a leper in a time of famine, it would be even worse to be a leper in a time of famine in the middle of a war. And if it were not bad enough to be a leper in a famine in a time of war, it would be even worse if your side was losing the war. Four lepers, locked outside their city. Four lepers who have been forgotten and abandoned by their own. Four lepers whose bodies are being eaten away by an incurable disease but whose minds are still sharp—at least sharp enough to understand their options.

There was only one option that had even the slightest prospect of life, and it was the option that required of them the greatest risk and the greatest courage. It would have been easier for them to surrender to a desperate situation, to curse God for all the sorrow he had let invade their lives, to despise their own people for abandoning them, and to give up and surrender themselves to death, but instead they surrendered themselves to life:

At dusk they got up and went to the camp of the Arameans. When they reached the edge of the camp, no one was there, for the Lord had caused the Arameans to hear the sound of chariots and horses and a great army, so that they said to one another, "Look, the king of Israel has hired the Hittite and Egyptian kings to attack us!" So they got up and fled in the dusk and abandoned their tents and their horses and donkeys. They left the camp as it was and ran for their lives.

The men who had leprosy reached the edge of the camp, entered one of the tents and ate and drank. Then they took silver, gold and clothes, and went off and hid them. They returned and entered another tent and took some things from it and hid them also.[3]

Hidden in this story is a promise and an insight to how God works in the world. The lepers went only to surrender to the Arameans, but God was doing what they could not do. He was giving them victory over the Arameans, but what the Arameans heard as the sounds of chariots and horses and a great army was actually the shuffling of four lepers coming out of hiding to appeal to the mercy of a merciless army. The lepers found what could not have been expected. In their fright, the Arameans left everything behind. Suddenly four homeless and hopeless lepers were the rulers of the wealth of an army.

It makes one wonder how many times we choose to remain in our desperation rather than allow it to drive us to the abundance that awaits us. And of this I am certain: whatever God has for us, whatever promises he longs to fulfill in our lives, whatever riches may await us, we will find them only when we choose to cross enemy lines and surrender ourselves to life. These four lepers were not satisfied to simply wait on death; they made an absurd and ridiculous decision to believe in the possibility that life was still waiting for them. And only after they acted did they discover that God was already acting on their behalf.

Sometimes we blame God for his lack of concern, while all the time what's missing is our urgency. We expect God to act but we never take responsibility to act ourselves, which is why so many of us never get down to that last arrow. We decide that playing it safe is the reasonable choice. We tell ourselves that only fools would believe that their best future would exist in a place of their greatest danger. What we can be certain of is that God is never apathetic. If there is apathy involved, it is ours. What in fact might be in play is that we haven't prepared to receive what God wants to give us. It is unfortunate, but far too often it is desperation that creates openness to the provision of God. And beyond a desperation for our own survival, we are best able to receive God's abundances when we move outside ourselves to the needs of others.

After the lepers had taken silver and gold and clothes and went and hid them for themselves, and as they were going tent by tent to see what else they could pillage, they stopped and looked at each other and knew that if this was the provision of God, this is not what God would have them do with it. They said to each other, "What we're doing is not right. This is a day of good news and we are keeping it to ourselves. If we wait until daylight, punishment will overtake us. Let us go at once and report this to the royal palace."[4]

So they went to the very people who had abandoned them, to the very king who had the gates locked after they were placed outside, and declared to them news that seemed too good to be true. And the news was not well received. After all, the invitation seemed terrifying: leave the safety of your fortress, open your doors, and step outside. If you stay where you are, you will die a slow and painful death. You will die of hunger and thirst. But in truth, what you will die of is fear. What you will find when you open the doors is that the battle has already been fought, the victory has already been won, and there is an abundance waiting for you, provision made ready; all you need to do is act like your life depends on it.

Fear is like a leprosy that eats away at our souls, and it will lead us to build fortresses that look like security and safety. Fear convinces us that we have locked out the dangers that would befall us, all the while blinding us to the fact that it hasn't locked the world out at all. Instead, fear has trapped us inside itself. It was never a fortress; it was always a prison.

Everything changes once you have stepped into life. Everything changes once you've experienced the goodness of God. Everything changes once you see how the universe is designed for abundance and not for scarcity. It not only changes the condition of your life but it changes you.

I love how four lepers who had every reason to never care about anyone looked at each other in a moment when the most profound epiphany came to all their minds. When we step out of death into life, there is no waiting for daylight. To hide what we have found, to hoard what we have been freely given, would be the greatest crime, an incurable leprosy of the soul. If for no other reason, we need to choose our most heroic lives, because a world desperately needs to see what it looks like to be fully alive. What the world needs most from you is for you to be fully alive. You and I, we needed proof of life to find life, and now we must be proof of life to those desperately searching for it.

MOVEMENT IS LIFE

Whether you are a king who has had the resources to build a fortress to protect yourself or a leper who has found yourself alone and desperate, you need to stop waiting for someone to make your life count. You need to act. You need to act as if your life depends on it, because it does. Life is action. Only the dead stay still. Life is movement; movement is life. You need to realize that whatever choices you make, no matter how much you accomplish, one thing is certain: all of our lives will end. That is not in question. It's the unavoidable reality of being human. The question still remains: Will you choose to live, or will you just lie there until death takes you?

But if you follow the story of the lepers carefully, you will know that what is at stake is so much more than just you. The only way you will ever act as if your life depends on it is if you realize that the lives of others depend on whether or not you act. The story of the four lepers could have ended way before it did. Certainly the story of four lepers who became the owners of the wealth of a city would more naturally fit the common narratives of a materialism far too many of us have embraced.

Because the lepers had nothing, it should not surprise anyone that when the opportunity came, they tried to take everything. They did what most of us would do. They satisfied their hunger and thirst, they ate and drank and pillaged the Aramean camp, and they were overtaken by their own fear and perhaps a greed that had not previously been given an opportunity to reveal itself.

They began hoarding everything they found and hiding it so that it could not be taken from them. At first they took what they needed, and then they took far more than they needed, all along thinking of no one but themselves. After all, they must have felt justified. No one had ever cared about them, no one made provision for them, no one cared whether they lived or died, no one acted on their behalf, so why should they care about anyone else? I don't think they made a conscious choice not to think about others. I think at first they were so consumed by their own good fortune that they thought about no one but themselves.

I am convinced, though, that even the worst of us, in our worst moments, have an inner voice that calls us to an unexpected nobility. I am convinced this is the voice of God. It was almost as if the lepers had this epiphany of conscience: *What we are doing is not right.* But it wasn't really wrong; all they were doing was enjoying their good fortune and embracing God's provision in their lives. Frankly, if this story ended here, it would better parallel the dominant teaching that is popularly taught as the gospel of prosperity. After all, the Scriptures are full of promises of God's goodwill and intention toward our lives. There are many places where God speaks of his desire and intention to bring prosperity and even abundance into our lives. Perhaps the most familiar are the words of Jeremiah in which God reminds us, "I know the plans I have for you, . . . plans to prosper you and not to harm you, plans to give you hope and a future."[5]

This belief system has spread across the world, fastest among the poor. It shouldn't surprise us that those who are in the most desperate of conditions are most desperate to believe there is an abundance waiting for them if they simply trust God to provide. The great problem with distortions of the truth is that they are distortions of the *truth*. And there is so much truth upon which this distortion is built. God is for us. He desires to bless our lives and even to prosper us. His plans and intentions toward us are always far greater than our own. If we ask him, he will take us on journeys that go beyond whatever we could ask for or imagine.

The problem, of course, is that God's assurance of provision for our lives is not a promise that everyone has great wealth awaiting them. The abundance that Jesus speaks of when he promises abundant life is far richer than any item we could ever buy or possession we could ever own. Sometimes we become angry with God because he never gives us what we expect of him. Still, for others of us, there's a more critical understanding. Somewhere the assumption was made that when God does guide us to great wealth, when he provides for us beyond our wildest imaginations, this prosperity is supposed to be the end of the story.

But even for four lepers who stumbled onto an endless wealth of resources left to them when God had driven out their enemies, the story was never intended to end there. The four lepers didn't have a script to follow, but they had a clear understanding of who God was and how he worked in the world. They knew there was no way in the world that God would provide so much only for them to hoard it. They knew they had become recipients of God's goodness and that they could not keep it for themselves. There is nothing wrong with enjoying the abundance God has given you, but there is something terribly wrong when you think everything God has given you he gave you with only you in mind.

Today we tend to focus so much on what we're supposed to do with our lives and how we can maximize our gifts and talents and potential. I have met so many people whose deepest struggles are about discovering their own destinies. At first I didn't see it, but after a time, the pattern became clear. We want God to prosper us. We want him to give us abundant lives. We want God to make our dreams come true. We know we have talent. We feel there is greatness within us waiting to be awakened. We have endless opportunities, yet somehow we feel paralyzed. It's as if all this God-given capacity is jammed up deep inside us. And we are confounded with this unsolvable puzzle of why we would want God to do more. It feels as if we have become less, which provokes an interesting question: Can we be less than a leper left in the desert in the middle of a war waiting to die? And the answer is yes. It's a tragic yes. We can become hoarders who make sure that no one else can take what has been given to us.

The last arrow moves you past what God will do *for* you to what God will do *through* you. The last arrow strikes only when we must act not only as if our lives depend on it but as if the lives of others depend on it as well. Too many of us act as though we have all the time in the world, while the world is desperately running out of time. As long as we are living for ourselves, we are still wandering in the darkness of the night. When you strike the last arrow, you have decided that there's no waiting for daylight.

I love the surprise that is found in this story: four lepers whose highest ambition was to survive and live one more day found themselves the benefactors who provided a future for a hopeless people. When you act like your life depends on it, you will discover that your life was never intended to be only about you. When you choose to live, you become a source of life. It may be your risk, but it's never only your reward. The tragedy of a life that is never fully lived is not solely the loss of that one life. The tragedy is the endless number of lives that would have been forever changed if we had chosen to live differently. The call to live your most heroic life isn't so that you can sit back at the end of the day and know that you are a hero. In fact, the most heroic lives are lived by those who never think of themselves but only of those for whom they have given their lives.

WHERE HEROES COME FROM

I met Luciano Meirelles in São Paulo, Brazil. I was struck by both his warmth and his intelligence. Luciano should have become a tragic statistic of abuse and abandonment. Even as he shared his story with me, he began with the disclaimer that he knew his story is not uncommon. I assure you it is. His mother was a heroin addict and was pregnant with Luciano when she was just a teenager. Her addiction was so severe that she kept using drugs even during her pregnancy. Those who knew his mother did not expect her baby to come to term, and the likelihood that the child would be born with huge birth defects and insurmountable physical and mental disabilities was almost certain. His father was a drug dealer and user as well, and this man's self-destructive behavior provided no protection for Luciano or his mother. When Luciano was born, the only people in the room were the mother who gave him birth and his father's mother, who came in spite of the fact that the entire family had chosen to disown them. His father did not bother to come. Most of his family did not bother to come. The room was practically empty.

When Luciano came into the world, that room was symbolic of what he would find when he took his first breath. He was alone. The first two years of his life, his drug-addicted parents took care of him—if that expression can be used in any way to describe the world in which he lived. Luciano was not simply undernourished, but there were many days when he would go entirely unfed, unattended, uncared for. It was no small miracle that Luciano lived past his second birthday. His father disappeared and essentially became a stranger to him. His mother was assassinated when he was twelve years old. When his father's parents could no longer bear to see the life this small boy had been born into, they stepped in and offered to adopt Luciano. He had a father and a mother, but he'd never really had parents, and now, strangely, his grandparents would become his parents. Even with a loving family, a place he could actually call home, it would be unlikely that Luciano would ever overcome the deep wounds and the unbearable trauma of his childhood.

As a teenager, Luciano chose to leave home and make his own way in the world. When he was twenty-one, he married his sweetheart, Cintia, who at the time was only nineteen. I remember how, when we were driving together, he quietly expressed that he felt certain the pain and scars of his childhood had a direct effect on the quality of his work and his personal capacity as a businessman. When I first engaged with Luciano while I was in Rio de Janeiro, he was in the midst of one of the most complicated business negotiations of his life. Behind the scenes, the son of a heroin addict was negotiating the complexities of the 2014 World Cup, and in a time of political and economic turbulence, he was able to host one of the greatest events in the world.

I can't quite put my finger on what Luciano does for a living; I just know that it requires him to fly to Geneva, Switzerland, to Chicago, Illinois, and to São Paulo, Brazil, not to mention other parts of Europe and South Africa. My best explanation is that he is both a serial entrepreneur and a strategic consultant to the highest tier of leaders in the world. He is unbelievably self-effacing, and one would be hard pressed to ever get him to talk about his accomplishments, much less his acquisitions. But when I asked him how many jobs around the world he would estimate he has been a part of creating, he thought for a moment and rounded the number to thirty thousand.

We might treat the story of four lepers who find themselves with enough wealth to save an entire city as an inspirational fable that has no basis in reality, and yet I know one of those four lepers.

His name is Luciano Meirelles. Who would have ever guessed that saving the life of this one small boy in São Paulo, Brazil, would one day provide the livelihood for thirty thousand people across the world?

A KING'S PORTION

You need to act like your life depends on it, because it's never just your life involved. You need to never settle for less because the world desperately needs everything you can bring to the table. Be careful of embracing the type of spirituality that has a deep disdain for ambition and hides apathy behind a language of simplicity. If you want to live a simple life, that's a beautiful thing. If you want to use it as an excuse to live beneath your God-given capacity, that is negligence.

I have always thought it was odd that people who can create wealth would consider it more spiritual to choose a life of poverty. Poor people don't choose to be poor. Those who are trapped in poverty do not choose to be trapped in poverty. We do not help the world by choosing to be less or do less; we help the world by choosing to be more and give more. There is no virtue in being given ten talents but choosing to be satisfied with living as if we had only one talent.

Remember that Elisha was angry with King Jehoash because he struck the arrow only three times. I wonder how many of us will find ourselves in a conversation with the Creator of the universe asking us, "Why did you settle for less? Why did you allow your weaknesses to define who you are? Why didn't you act as if your life depended on it? Why did you give up on life? Why did you give up on me?" You can almost hear the echoes of Elisha's voice: "Why did you stop striking the arrow?" Stop bemoaning your circumstances. Stop drowning in your despair. Stop using your present crisis as an excuse to shrink back from the challenge before you. Pick up the arrow and strike!

A leper is more powerful than a king if the leper is stepping into the life God created him to live and the king is not. And though they seem to live in completely different worlds, the leper and the king are connected. We are all connected. We need to act as though our lives depend on it, because everything is connected and everything we do matters. We feel this interconnection when someone else's life affects our lives, and we feel it when someone else's choices directly affect our choices, but more often than not we underestimate how our lives affect the lives of others.

COLLATERAL BEAUTY

My friend Luciano Meirelles asked if I would speak at an art exhibition introducing his daughter Deborah to the art world in the United States. She was only seventeen years old and had already been accepted by five of the most prestigious art schools in the world. Soon she would be headed to Parsons Paris to join an elite selection of artists who had been identified as the best in the world.

It struck me how far removed his daughter's world is from his mother's world. To describe Deborah's work as astonishing is an understatement. Her work is both imaginative and precise; her art is both provocative and profound. It's hard to wrap your head around the level of skill and talent that can be contained in a seventeen-year-old.

I asked Luciano when it was discovered that Deborah had this extraordinary talent. He said it was only two years earlier, when she was fifteen. Luciano and Cintia told Deborah that they all would be moving from Southern California back to São Paulo. Imagine telling a fifteen-year-old she has to leave California and all of her friends, all the places she'd come to know and love. Deborah would describe herself in that moment as unspeakably angry. And while her father was trying to explain to her why they needed to go back together as a family, she was frantically and feverishly doodling on a napkin, using it as a way of venting her anger and disapproval. When the conversation was over, her father saw the napkin and decided to put it in his pocket and keep it.

He later asked her how long she had been doing things like this, and she said not long. He said, "You know, this is really good," and she responded that it was nothing. It's just something she did while she was angry. Then an opportunity—or a problem, depending on how you look at it—arose in her life. She had a friend who was housebound because he could not walk and did not have a wheelchair. The wheelchair would cost around $5,000, and Deborah desperately wanted to help make this happen for him.

Then her father came up with the opportunity. A boat show was going to be taking place and the owner, having seen some of Deborah's sketches, offered to create a gallery there where she could sell her work. She made ten pieces of art in just a matter of days, and when the show was over, she had made $20,000. This was the first time anyone had seen her work publicly. This was the first time she had ever tried to sell a piece. With that $20,000, she was more than able to buy her friend's wheelchair, and with the rest of it, she funded two humanitarian projects in different parts of the world. Already at seventeen she was seeing her art not simply as a way of expressing her own inner narrative or expressing her own God-given talent but as a vehicle to do good in the world. For Deborah, art is more than something God has given her for her own fulfillment; art is a resource that she has been entrusted with and a vehicle through which she can make the world a better place.

The son of an addict becomes the father of an artist. Born into a world of drug dealers, he gives birth to a world of dealers of hope. There is no way possible that Luciano, when he was seventeen years old, could have seen how the choices he was making would affect his yet-to-be-born daughter when she was seventeen years old. But we're all connected and our choices are never only our own. They affect everyone around us and also have an effect on those yet to come.

It would be nice if we could see the future. It would have been so much easier for those four lepers if they could have seen the

Aramean camp abandoned. It would have required so much less of them if they could have known beforehand that there was an abundance awaiting them. It would have made it so much easier if they had just known that God had prepared the way. We don't get that luxury.

The future reveals itself only when it becomes the present. This is why it's so important to act as if your life depends on it. Your actions have momentum. Every action has a reaction; every choice ushers in a future. If you just sit there, if you just stand around and hope that the world will get better, if you settle for what is because what you long for demands too much of you, then this thing called life will always seem elusive to you. Existence is a slow death; mediocrity is like quicksand that slowly consumes you and sucks the life out of you. What will it take to create in you a sense of urgency? What conditions or circumstances will be necessary for you to finally refuse to surrender to death and make the hard choice to live? Most of us know it's spiritual to pray, but somehow we miss the fact that it's just as spiritual to act.

SEARCHING FOR REFUGE

The last family I met while we were in the Bekáa Valley was headed by a fifty-five-year-old Syrian woman who looked as if she were in her eighties. Her husband had been killed before they left Damascus, and the father of her grandchildren had gone to Germany more than two years before and they had not heard from him since. All the other relatives had been taken hostage, imprisoned, or executed. She was alone in the middle of this interim settlement with three grandchildren all under the age of ten. She told her story through her tears, and on occasion her words were unintelligible as weeping overwhelmed her and her sorrow seemed to consume all the oxygen from her lungs.

We left when we heard the call to prayer. She was a devout Muslim, specifically a Sunni Muslim, and we wanted to respect her desire to pray and ask God for help. We left quietly, and though the children were a beautiful delight, I was overwhelmed with sorrow myself. The reality of their condition was sobering, to say the least. They had no hope, no way out, no future that any human being would ever want for themselves or anyone they loved, and we were walking away, returning to our amazing lives, returning to all of our creature comforts, to all of the provisions that we would thank God for.

As we walked, I quietly asked the representative from the humanitarian agency we were working with if I could help this family in just a small way. I knew it was against policy and procedures. I knew that it would be inappropriate to give them money directly and that we needed to respect the process, but I just couldn't shake the fact that in my pocket was more money than the family would see in three months. I was holding within feet of them enough money to buy them food and supplies that would otherwise never come their way. The worker's response was as I expected. He graciously thanked me for my good intention but reminded me that it would violate the process they had implemented for long-term engagement of the refugees.

I might have asked two or three more times—I don't remember. I told him I knew that making the gift wasn't going to solve the problem and that maybe my desire to do this was more about what I needed to give than what they needed to receive. I actually reconciled myself to the belief that I was not going to be able to give them money, until another of the workers came to me and said, "Let's go take a walk." He must have seen the despair in my eyes and sensed that I was close to having a meltdown. So we walked back to the temporary shelter that this family of four lived in. The grandmother was already in her time of prayer. I didn't know what would be appropriate, or maybe I knew but I didn't care. I had the children interrupt her and ask her if I could speak to her for just a moment. She had changed clothes from the clothes she wore when we'd interviewed her. She was wearing all white out of reverence to God.

Through the translator, I expressed these simple words to her: "Sometimes you pray and sometimes you're the answer to prayer." Then I handed her the small amount of money I had. I asked that God would bless her, and I left, never to see them again.

I am more than aware that I did not solve the Syrian refugee crisis. I didn't even solve it for this one family. But it doesn't change the truth of that moment. Sometimes we pray; sometimes we are the answers to prayer. You become the answer to prayer when you act as though your life depends on it. Because it does. And so do the lives of everyone your life touches.

STAND YOUR GROUND

Though I had traveled to the Middle East many times, the first trip in which I took my entire family was in 2001 to Beirut, Lebanon. On that trip we were specifically there to spend time with a family that had become dear to us. Nabil and Mimi Khoury were part of our community in Los Angeles before they moved to Beirut. Mimi worked as my personal assistant, and then she met Nabil at a conference on Christian-Muslim relationships. Nabil was Lebanese and had a unique concern and passion for the Muslims in his country. Mimi always had a deep concern for the Middle East and a great love for Islamic peoples.

In 2001 they were two young parents who would soon be raising four small boys. And while many of us are used to the creature comforts that our lives in the Western world allot us, Mimi and Nabil lived on the fifth floor of a Beirut apartment complex where there was very little room for all of them in the place they called home.

Many people come and go when it comes to humanitarian

work or serving in the more difficult places in the world, but Mimi and Nabil were lifers. They had a deep intention to not only serve in Beirut but also become an integral part of their community. Our church community in Los Angeles decided to do something we had never done for anyone before: we decided to build them a house. I told Mimi and Nabil to find a plot of land and we would build their future home.

If you are building a house in a suburb in the United States, you might factor in such things as where the best schools are or what kind of neighborhood you want to raise your kids in. For Mimi and Nabil, the question was far more significant. Lebanon is sliced into pieces by religious and cultural divides. There are areas where the Druze live and areas where the Sunnis live. There are the areas for the Shiites and then areas for the Christians. And although there may be some variation on the theme, you do not move, generally speaking, to the Sunni area if you're a Christian, and you do not move to the Christian area if you are a Shiite. You don't even cross lines if you're Druze in another expression of the Islam faith. Everyone has their neighborhood based on their beliefs. Lebanon is a nation divided by religion. So you might imagine the controversy that arose among those who were close to them in Lebanon when Mimi and Nabil decided they would build a house located on a hill that was for years a battleground fortified with military bunkers and multiple trenches running through it. It was the intersection of the Christian, Catholic, and Islamic communities.

When the couple brought me the blueprints for the house, it

was so modest and functional. I think they were surprised that this house would not do and that we would not invest our money in a house that would be so limiting to their work. We commissioned them to come back with a plan in which we could build a home for them that would reflect their value of hospitality. We wanted them to have a place where they could share their lives with the many people they cared about so deeply.

By 2006 that house was finally completed. Mimi, Nabil, and their four boys had a home and a place to offer refuge for those looking for hope and meaning. For Nabil and Mimi, buying that plot of land and building their home was choosing to decline the security of surrounding themselves with a community of Christians. Instead, they were risking their lives to make a more profound declaration that although they were not Muslims, the Muslim people were their community, their friends, their neighbors, their family. The fact that this family chose this particular plot of land poignantly expressed to the world around them, *It's right here that we take a stand.* The very place where they poured the concrete for their driveway was the ground where the Israeli tanks positioned themselves over a hill to shower the ground beneath them with bombs and artillery fire.

Almost as soon as the house was finished and they'd had the grand opening, Beirut was at war again. I was in Los Angeles watching CNN while calling Nabil in Beirut to see if they were safe. It was surreal to be standing on their patio with Nabil more than ten years later as he told the story from his perspective, almost laughing as if there were a comedic element to it. He explained, "Erwin, this is where I was standing, overlooking the city, when you called me from Los Angeles. I remember you saying, 'Nabil, I can see the bombs dropping on the city of Beirut.'" And he laughed and said, "Yes, you are watching them on television. I was watching the exact same bombs drop as I stood on my patio."

Their friends and loved ones who lived deeper in the Christian communities appealed to Nabil and Mimi to leave as quickly as possible, yet they refused to leave even while both their home and their lives were in danger. Only after the heavy aerial bombardment of the Shiite neighborhoods intensified, literally shaking their home every night, and after everyone in their neighborhood began to move toward a frantic search for shelter, did they leave as well. Nabil casually explained that their exit strategy was always that they would take two cars and divide their family in half. That way, if one of their cars was hit by an explosive, the children who remained had at least one parent to raise them. The fifth-story apartment where they had previously lived was struck by a bomb and nearly destroyed. The house where they had defied common sense and religious boundaries, and instead decided to take their stand, remains standing to this day.

If you are going to live the life that God created you to live, if you are going to live to your full potential, if you are going to live the kind of life that never settles, you have to come to a place where you decide to stop running and instead choose to take a stand. And I am not talking about taking a stand on issues or dogmas or beliefs—

those things come and go and are often circumstantial. Here what it means to take a stand is far more profound and central to who you are. You have to eventually stop trying to be what everyone else wants you to be, and you have to stop choosing to become only what comes easy to you. You have to decide what will define you. What will mark you as a person? How will you be known by others? Your decisions are the direct result of truly knowing yourself.

Frankly, I think most of us live our lives in fear. Who we become is less the result of where we are going than it is the consequence of what we are running from. It's unfortunate, but I completely resonate with this. I wish I didn't. I wish I could say that my life has never been defined by my fears. I wish I could say that my life has not been affected by what I was running from and that all of my life has been completely attributed to what I was running toward. But sadly I'm like most people when it comes to fear. Courage is a rare and precarious possession.

STAND APART

The prophet Samuel, who lived in the time of King David, described the unique individuals who came to David's side and created a fierce alliance with him. He went into more detail about three particular individuals, and with each one he told a story that serves as the résumé for their leadership. The third is a man named Shammah. Samuel described one brief moment when the Philistines banded together at a place where there was a field full of lentils, and Israel's troops fled from them in fear. But Shammah took his stand in the middle of the field. He defended it and struck the Philistines down. And we are told, of course, that the Lord brought about a great victory.[1]

As I picture the incident in my mind, the imagery is like a scene straight out of *Gladiator,* with cinematography that's a combination of Ridley Scott and Terrence Malick. An ominous Philistine army gathers at the edge of a field of lentils. The Israelites see them and are overwhelmed with fear. The Philistines are imposing both in stature and in sheer numbers. These are the people of Goliath. They are warriors by nature. They are ruthless and seemingly fearless. The Israelites, on the other hand, are clearly not ready for war. Just the sight of the Philistines causes them to abandon their posts. They run for their lives.

Ironically, running in fear is not a solution to their problem. The Philistines are going to come, and eventually there will be war, which is a reminder for our own lives. When we run in fear, we're only postponing the inevitable. We will eventually have to face those fears. We will eventually have to fight those battles. Running only makes us weaker and makes our opposition stronger.

But then there is Shammah, who stands between two armies: one that came to fight and the other running in fear. Maybe at first he finds himself running with his men. Maybe at first he thinks it is a strategic retreat in an attempt to reposition so that they can engage the enemy with some advantage. But then there is a moment when Shammah realizes that, for his army, the battle has already been lost.

I can only imagine the satisfaction that must fill the Philistines when they realize that the battle is over before it ever began. How strange it must be when suddenly they see one man stop and turn around. Maybe Shammah does it only after pleading in vain with his men to take a stand. Maybe it is in that moment when he realizes that all his appeals to their honor and duty are to no avail. Maybe it is when he finds himself alone that he finds his courage. Suddenly the Philistines see one man stop and turn around. Shammah stands alone against an army. He stops in the middle of a field of lentils and takes his stand.

Perhaps at first the Philistines simply send out one soldier, their champion, to face Shammah and end his insolence. And then, to their shock and dismay, Shammah strikes him down. Perhaps then they send three, and then ten, and then eventually however many of their men have a thirst for blood. They rush through the field of lentils to win a war against an army of one.

Who can know the mind of this one man? How can we call his action anything but madness? How could a person have such little value for his own life that he would choose a battle he could never win? No one would scorn him for running. After all, he would simply be joining a legion of cowards who would together weave a story of impossible odds justifying their cowardice.

People like Shammah create a problem for the rest of us. One person who chooses to live a heroic life disrupts the narrative "We are living a lesser life" as the acceptable option. Even if Shammah had failed, even if he had died, the moment he took a stand, he changed the story. He changed the standard. It's hard to tell the story as you sit around the fireplace and explain that you had no option but to run, because some innocent child will ask, "But where's Shammah?"

For Shammah, there is no point in running for your life if once you get there you have no reason to live. And if his stubbornness doesn't make things bad enough, the outcome makes it worse. He not only survives but he wins! He does by himself what the armies of Israel did not believe they could do together. God does through one man what he clearly longed to do through all of his people. If they had not run in fear, Shammah's story would have been *their* story. When Shammah returns to his people, battle weary and covered in the blood of his enemies, there is really nothing he needs to say. His presence, his very existence, is an indictment on every other man who fled. Don't expect to be popular if you choose to rise above the status quo.

I have to wonder, what was it about that particular field of lentils that inspired Shammah to take a stand? Maybe it was just the intersection of two armies that brought him to that place, or maybe that field of lentils was a marker of the food and resources his people would need to have to survive. There was no explanation for why that particular place. Maybe it's because that's not nearly as important as the point of it all. There comes a time and a place where you have to decide, *This is worth fighting for. This is where I stand. This is who I am. This is the life I have chosen.*

I will not run. I will not allow fear to move me from where I should be to where it wants me to live. I would rather die facing the challenge than exist running from it.

The stark reality is that all of us choose a burial plot long before we're buried in the ground. All of us, whether consciously or unconsciously, find a piece of ground where we choose to take our stand. Yet the reality is that for far too many of us, the place where we set our feet is rarely the result of a decisive decision to stop running and start fighting.

A FUTURE WORTH FIGHTING FOR

I've always been drawn to conspiracy theories. I was a huge fan of *The X-Files*, featuring two characters named Mulder and Scully. I was more than excited when I heard the producers were bringing them back in a feature film years ago, but I was surprised by the narrative they chose to advance. In the end, it made perfect sense. And even though I loved so much about the stories that the show's brilliant creator, Chris Carter, told, it was extremely disappointing that their final declaration was "Fight the future." If nothing else, these three words ensured there could be no satisfying end to their story. If all of your efforts are given to this one task of fighting the future, failure is nothing but certain. Carter's world was the perfect scenario for every person who struggles with paranoia. It was a plot that twisted together government conspiracies, alien invasions, and monsters that haunt our deepest fears and darkest imaginations. In Carter's world, the future was bleak and there was little we could do to change it.

Mulder and Scully's world was filled with conspiracies. In their world dark forces were at work and could not be stopped. For them the future was bleak and ominous. All they could do was fight the future rather than fight *for* the future. To fight for the future, we must have hope. We must believe there is a future worth fighting for. We simply can't fight the future. The future is coming whether we like it or not. In fact, there is nothing we can do to stop it from coming. This doesn't mean we are powerless when it comes to the future, but it does mean we have to take a different stance toward engaging it.

You can't fight the future, but you can create the future. To fight the future is to ensure that you will be lost and left behind to the past. For some, the idea of standing your ground is a desperate resolution to find some way to make sure that the past is the future and that the future never happens. Frankly, the apocalyptic tone of the Christian faith has postured the church as an enemy of the future. The faithful hold on to the past and fight the future. If I have had one struggle in my faith journey, it has been that the church seems to march into the future walking backward. For many, the only hope of faith is that one day we will leave this earth and be free from a future that filled us with fear. Often our best hope has been that Jesus would come back soon. Yet I am convinced this is exactly the wrong viewpoint for any of us who live by faith. Faith is the fuel of the future, and if God is the God of yesterday, today, and tomorrow, then tomorrow should fill us with inexplicable hope. No matter how bleak the present may seem for those of us who believe, the future is always full of hope.

TRAPPED IN TIME

It's a surreal experience to cross the borders of nations that not only have distinct geographic locations but are also expressions of different times in history. Most of us live with the delusion that the whole world is traveling at the same point in time and that today means the same thing for everyone on the planet. For many of us who live with the delusion that we are on the front end of history, it will come as a tremendous shock when we visit Tokyo and realize that the technology that is common to them does not even exist for us. The opposite is true as well. When we walk the streets of Damascus or travel throughout Cambodia, we realize there are entire societies across the world still traveling through periods of history that we only read about in books. For some places in the world, the Industrial Revolution is the next great cultural advancement of their society. It's hard to imagine the mind-sets in the Middle East that allow tribal wars and religious factions to justify violence and terrorism. The reality, though, is that fifteen hundred years ago, our ancestors saw the world in very similar ways.

Time is not only relative; it is relative to geography as well. It was almost as if the clock had been magically turned backward to 1965 when I landed in Havana, Cuba. My iPhone suddenly became a new technological application. Press "Camera" and take a photograph of what the world looked like fifty years ago. (Wouldn't that be a cool app? We could set the date 1517 and our photographs would show us the world in an earlier time.) Four months after my birth, the Cuban revolution took place, and at just about the time I was migrating from El Salvador to the United States, Fidel Castro was firmly established as the leader of what would be described as a socialist republic. Cuba would remain as one of the world's last countries following the Marxist-Leninist ideology. Their constitution describes the Communist party of Cuba as the leading force of society and of the state.

Living in Miami from 1965 to 1974, I experienced the massive migration of Cuban refugees firsthand. Castro's regime and the militant implementation of its socialist ideology created a mass exodus of Cuba's intellectual and creative class. Families and friends were divided; loved ones would never see each other again; and in the span of one lifetime, two different worlds were created out of one people. The Cuban migration transformed Miami into what has become known as Little Havana. The Cuban people have experienced tremendous prosperity even though they escaped with nothing but their lives. Those who were left behind were trapped within the borders of the small island we know as Cuba. For them, it was a very different story; it was as if the world stood still. While fifty years have passed, it was as if a hammer crashed against the clock that measured time, and for them the world stopped the moment their freedom was lost.

It was surreal walking the streets of a city where the transportation seemed to have been resourced by a Hollywood film company. I live in the city that knows how to re-create the past, but now I was walking a city that *chose* to stay in the past. I could see with my own eyes the tragic effect of making a stand by holding on to the past and fighting against the future. As romantic and magical as it was to be able to travel across this country trapped in a time long forgotten, it also became for me a harsh reminder that all of us are in danger of losing the future if we hold on to the past. It was inconvenient to be in a place where there is no Internet, no e-mails, no texting, no contact with the outside world, but those inconveniences soon gave way to the realization that there are beautiful people there who also see their lives as having no future, no freedom, and no hope.

So my question for you is this: When you stand your ground, are you fighting the future or fighting *for* the future?

VIVA LA LIBERTAD

I had arrived in Cuba with three other men I had just met who had been working in Cuba for many years. One of the first people I met in Havana was an amiable and charismatic man in his late seventies. He introduced himself as Luis, our driver and tour guide for the few days we would be traveling across Cuba. We stood in the parking lot outside of the Aeropuerto Internacional José Martí and had our first experience of socialist efficiency. We waited there for about

three hours for our rental car, which took no small amount of negotiations. Luis had a car, but he was not permitted to put outsiders in
his vehicle. During the hours while we waited, he would point to
the various vehicles where military personnel surveyed us and
waited for the slightest infraction to justify detaining us.

Because we had a lot of time on our hands, we began having
a wonderful conversation to get to know each other. At first Luis
was hesitant to share his story, but after a while, when he assessed
our genuine interest, he became an open book. He proceeded to
tell me a story far more fascinating than one I could have ever
made up. He was Fidel Castro's right-hand man for almost all of
his adult life. He was a colonel in the military and was solely responsible for the safety and security of the president himself. His
decades of service for Castro took him to more than forty countries around the world, and there was perhaps no person in all of
Castro's administration who was more trusted than himself. If
Castro ever became the victim of injury or needed a blood trans-
fusion, Luis was the only person in the world authorized to give
blood to save Castro's life. His term of service ended abruptly one
day when he was brought into the president's office and accused of
treason. Without trial or evidence, he was thrown into the harsh-
est prison for the next two years of his life.

When I tried to understand what could have caused such a
drastic turn of events, the pieces just never fit. Even years later,
long after this injustice had befallen him, he was still a man of
honor and refused to blame anyone. But there was a strange

coincidence of circumstances that those around him would point to.

It seemed that the colonel was essentially an irreligious man throughout his entire life, while his beautiful wife was a person of deep faith. His idealism and faith were deeply rooted in the promises of Marx and Castro. For most of Luis's life, the teachings of Jesus were irrelevant to his life and certainly not an expected part of his future. Then unexpectedly what he had never been open to finally broadened his mind and heart. Maybe it was a coincidence, maybe it was just an odd alignment of circumstances, but shortly after his declaration of faith in Jesus and his public baptism identifying himself with the Savior of the world, both of these choices gave him a freedom he had never known and cost him all the freedom he had ever known.

Not once in our conversations did I sense even a twinge of bitterness or regret. In fact, Luis was a constant encouragement and inspiration to us all. I wasn't sure if we had gone to Cuba to help him or if he was simply waiting there to help us. What was clear was that he was a man who stood his ground, who decided what his life would be about, who knew that it would be easier to run but instead he found himself in a field of lentils and decided, *This is where I stand.* I felt certain, even as we said our good-byes, that I had just met a man who was holding his last arrow. Within the confines of what we would consider limited freedom, he was living a life that was truly free.

I didn't know what to expect while we were in Cuba. I was the guest of a former Major League Baseball player whose platform as a world-class pitcher opened up a world that was closed for so many others. If the principle is to stand one's ground, here was a man who literally made his life doing that very thing. He would walk up to a mound, hold a ball in his hand, and throw it nearly a hundred miles an hour, challenging his opponent to hit it if he could.

The psychology of pitching is fascinating to me. To do it at the highest level, you have to have a particular mind-set. It's you against the world. You want the ball in your hand; you want the game to rest on your shoulders. Pitchers are commanders. When they walk on that mound, their full intention is to rule from that perch. Pitchers take a stand, face their opponents, and love that the prospect of victory relies on them. The possibility of defeat does not elude them; it just does not dissuade them. They will of course lose sometimes, but they decide they can live with that because they can only know victory if they risk defeat. It is this mind-set that is necessary to strike the last arrow. If you don't get on the mound, you'll never throw a strike. If you never throw a strike, you'll never get the win.

So it shouldn't surprise me that the first pastor we met in Cuba was a former pitcher as well. There is a national church there, but like so many places in the world, the official church is not nearly as powerful as the unofficial one. There is something renegade about the movement of Jesus. It does not conform well to the rules and regulations imposed upon it by governments or institutions. The most powerful expressions of the movement of Jesus are always underground or outside the mainstream. We had the wonderful experience of being guests of a beautiful family who lived in a very humble home that had been subdivided between their residence and the place where their congregation gathered. I was there on an evening when people came from hours away, whether on bike or on foot, to worship together and be encouraged by their common faith.

I was there only to observe, but moments before the service, I was asked instead to bring a message. Although Spanish is my first language, it is definitely not my primary language. Believe me, my sense of inadequacy was at a peak and I could think of a thousand reasons to say no, but I knew that if I let this opportunity slip by, I would remember it as one of those moments I could never regain. After all, it's about striking the last arrow.

So in a horrific abuse of the Spanish language, I preached my guts out for thirty minutes to a crowd jam-packed in a garage overflowing into the street, where people stood in the rain to hear a message about Jesus. For me, it felt the same as speaking to twenty thousand people at an event that would be televised worldwide. There is something powerful about stepping into a moment that is bigger than you. I love the fact that after I was finished, the pastor looked at me and said, "What you just did was completely illegal." We both looked at each other and smiled with a deep sense of satisfaction.

It's nice to leave a place with an empty quiver, but it's far more powerful to walk next to those who every day of their lives strike the last arrow. Even in a country that has stolen its people's freedom, there are those who every day stand their ground and fight for their future. And in so many places where we have great freedom, we choose to live in fear and hold on to the past.

What we must answer for ourselves if we decide to never settle is, where have we chosen to take our stand? What is the plot of ground that will define our story? I know one thing for certain about all of us: we are all standing somewhere. But how did we get there and why are we there? Did we get there because we are running *away* from something or running *to* something? Do our feet mark where fear has driven us or where faith has taken us?

To stand our ground will look different for each of us. For my wife, Kim, it means getting on a plane and flying to Iraqi Kurdistan to stand with the hundreds of thousands of Kurdish refugees and see if she can help them have a place to stand. Here in LA, we chose to stand our ground on the corner of Hollywood Boulevard and La Brea Avenue. Three times this past year, we were forced to close down our Sunday gatherings due to bomb threats, but our fearless volunteers are undaunted.

The irony is that twenty years ago, when we made a decision to ensure that the church would have a presence in the middle of Hollywood, so many of the leaders in our faith were not at all hesitant to tell us that reaching Hollywood was a hopeless endeavor. And frankly, it is much easier to do the same work in the suburbs than it is to do it in the city and much easier to do it in virtually every other city than in the cities that need it most. Every time we open the doors to the building where Mosaic meets, I am reminded that today there are thousands of people who have chosen to take a stand. They are not fighting against Hollywood; they are fighting for Hollywood.

For me, Los Angeles is our field of lentils. If the church had not run from the cities, we would have never lost the cities.

SOMETHING NEW UNDER THE SUN

As I look back on my personal journey, the singular cause for me losing ground or giving up ground where I should have taken a stand has been fear. Sometimes it's been the fear of failure, sometimes it's been the fear of success, and quite often it's been the fear of rejection. If people have never known fear, they have never had a need for courage. I'm quite familiar with fear, and courage has been demanded of me more often than I have wanted.

Over a decade ago, I found myself pacing in our living room having a conversation with myself that Kim interrupted. I was at the end of myself. I felt as if I were going to explode if I didn't speak up about something about which I had chosen to remain silent. I said, "I can't keep quiet about it anymore. I need to say something. I know that Solomon was wrong. Solomon was wrong."

My wonderful wife, who has a master's degree in theology, was immediately troubled by my statement. "What are you talking about?" she pressed in.

I said, "When Solomon said there is nothing new under the sun, he was wrong. He was wrong. He was wrong."

Kim has a unique way of interacting with me, and when she heard what I said, her immediate response was "You are going to hell." Kim uses emphatic language. While I love how she just speaks her truth with that regard of consequence to my soul, her statement might be considered a bit harsh, or somewhat of the equivalent of blunt-force trauma. I know what she was hearing. When I was saying Solomon was wrong, she was hearing me say the Bible was wrong. I wasn't saying the Bible was wrong; I was saying that what Solomon said in the Bible was wrong.

She could see my intensity and felt very anxious. I sense that Kim has spent most of our marriage trying to help me fit into the way the rest of the world thinks. She feels deeply the pain of my lack of ability to conform. She began to implore, "Please don't say that outside of this house. Please keep that here. Say it to me if you need to, but please don't say it anywhere else."

Out of respect for Kim, I kept my convictions to myself for years. I just let it burn and seethe inside my soul. I traveled the world, and everywhere I went, wherever I encountered people of faith, it would almost always happen. As I began to introduce an idea or a thought, the response of the Christian thought leaders across the world was "Erwin, there is nothing new under the sun." This statement from Solomon had, from my perspective, become like a lethal virus that was killing the future of the church. After all, if there's nothing new under the sun, it gives us every justification to live in the past.

In 2008 I had been invited to speak at a conference where

more than ten thousand people were in attendance and where I could no longer remain silent. Honestly, I knew what it would cost me. I knew what it would do to my reputation, to my standing in the faith community. I understood that the accepted view of reality was that the words of Solomon were absolutely true and that to think differently was to go against the Scriptures. As expected, that was my last invitation from that conference. Even as I walked off the stage, I told my son that it was time for me to leave the public arena and move in a different direction with my life. For the next six years, I virtually disappeared from the world that I had come to know so well. I stopped writing books; I stopped speaking at conferences; I started a business; I focused on fashion and film. I gave myself to starting something new under the sun.

At the end of those six years, I was invited to speak at the Willow Creek Leadership Summit. I was asked to listen to the speakers during the three days and bring the closing message, wrapping up what I had heard over that time. And there it was again. I kept hearing it over and over and over, this prevailing theme that there is nothing new under the sun—that all there is to do is to do what has been done better than it has been done in the past. There was only one dissenting voice that stood out to me in the entire conference: a marketing guru named Seth Godin. He was perhaps the only speaker who was not of the Christian faith. It struck me that the only voice that spoke about the future as the result of a creative act was the one person whose view of reality was not shaped by this fixed view of the future.

Sitting next to me, my wife could feel my anxiety. Even moments before I spoke, she asked me what was wrong. Why did I seem so fidgety?

Let me be clear: I find no pleasure in accruing the disdain of others. I like to be liked. I love to be loved. And when I sensed in the depth of my soul that the very message I gave six years before that put me on the blacklist was the very message that I felt God was demanding I speak in this moment, it was the last thing I wanted to do. I wanted to give a message that would give me greater popularity. I wanted to bring a message that would inspire everyone and elevate my value. I think I wanted what all of us want.

And I can tell you that in those hours before I stepped onto that platform, I was having an intense conversation with God. I tried to remind him of how poorly it went six years before, in case he had forgotten. I tried to point out to him that my life did not get better but in fact became more difficult when I broached this subject to his people. I know it sounds crazy when we talk about hearing God's voice and having conversations with him as if he were a friend or familiar, but for me it was so clear. What I didn't hear from God was an empathetic appreciation for my present dilemma. What I heard so clearly was that he didn't really care whether people liked me or not and that it wasn't really his concern if the message would increase my popularity or end it altogether, but that all that should matter to me, because it's all that matters to him, is that I tell the truth.

And honestly, for me it was perplexing that what I believed

wasn't so clear to everyone. Yes, Solomon said there's nothing new under the sun, but he also said that everything is meaningless.[2] But everything isn't meaningless. Life can be full of meaning. It's only meaningless when our lives are absent of God. Yet when our lives are alive in God, our lives are full of meaning. Of course, there would be nothing new under the sun if we lived our lives apart from God, but we were never intended to live apart from him. We were always intended to live our lives with him, and with him there is always something new. In fact, that's what God says through Isaiah when he tells us,

> Forget the former things;
>> do not dwell on the past.
> See, I am doing a new thing!
>> Now it springs up; do you not perceive it?[3]

So who are we to believe: Solomon when he says there is nothing new under the sun, or God who says, "I am doing a new thing"? The same God who says, "I am making everything new!" the same God who tells us that he gives us a new heart and makes us new creations, the same God who calls us to sing a new song and whose mercies are new every morning.[4]

As I see it, the future is my field of lentils. I have found the church strangely walking backward into the future. The church has become an institution that preserves the past and fears the future. It is not an overstatement to say that the church has become more of a reflection of what we are running from than what we are running to. No wonder we have lost our power to change the world. No wonder the church has lost its magnetism to a world searching for hope. We are seen as the guardians of tradition. The church is known for fighting the future rather than creating the future that humanity desperately needs.

After eight years, I was invited to the very conference where I chose to first stand my ground and fight for the future of the church. It was astonishing to me that one of the most respected and trusted voices said casually during his session, "We've all heard it said that there's nothing new under the sun, and we all know that isn't true." I love that. We have all heard it said, and perhaps now we all know it's not true.

THE GOOD FIGHT

When I wrote my previous book, *The Artisan Soul*,[5] I knew I needed to stop in the field of lentils and fight, even if I must fight alone. The book is an anthropology on what it means to be human. A daring question for me was, what makes us uniquely human? At the core is the argument that every human being is both a work of art and an artist at work. Being created in the image of God is revealed in the creative nature of humanity. It's a simple declaration, but the implications are seismic: like bees create hives and ants create colonies, humans create futures. I know that thought is disturbing for good people of faith. After all, hasn't the future already been created? Isn't God the only one who has anything to do with the future? Isn't it insolent and arrogant to believe that we have anything to do with the creation of the future? And the problem, of course, is that this false view of reality allows us to abdicate our God-given responsibility.

Not a word of this book matters if your choices don't matter. But if your choices have any effect on the future at all, then you need to stand your ground. You need to decide to stop running in fear and turn around and fight the good fight. You need to decide who you are and what you are about, why you live and what you are willing to die for. Until you decide to stand your ground, you will live your life like a leaf blown by the wind. You will see yourself as a victim of circumstances or, even worse, of God's cruelty.

It's strange to me, but I know people who have already bought the plot of land in which they will be buried. When I have talked to them, this process was incredibly important to them. They carefully selected the view and the people who would surround them. How strange that there are people in this world who have taken more care to decide where they will die than how they will live. I knew a man whose uncle insisted that he be buried with a six-pack of beer in his casket. Strange what people want in their coffin with them. When I die, I want to make sure there are no arrows left to put by my dead body. I just want an empty quiver. And may you die with your quiver empty too.

8

FIND YOUR PEOPLE

O ne of the great privileges I have had in my life is to meet extraordinary people, the kind of people you read about or hear about on the news. If you're anything like me, those extraordinary individuals seem almost like a different species from whatever kind of creature we might be. Even if I am afforded only a moment in their presence, I want to learn everything I can and do everything possible to absorb every aspect of their beings. I imagine I am hoping that their greatness is contagious, that it will somehow transfer from them to me, kind of the way it did with Elijah to Elisha. Certain people stand out to me because of either their undeniable intelligence, creative genius, incomparable warmth and kindness, or matchless energy.

There is always something about them that strikes you as unforgettable. From Tony Blair to Colin Powell, from FDR to JFK, to business icons like Richard Branson or social entrepreneurs like Blake Mycoskie (TOMS Shoes), there's always a sense that they are a different level of human being whose greatness is singular and self-contained. When we look more closely, though, we begin to realize that there's something far more powerful at work. Although we see them as singular expressions of greatness, they are in fact more than that. They are the visible manifestation of a far greater reality. They are individuals who represent a whole.

While it is undeniable that they accomplished great things, they did not accomplish those great things alone. In fact, the contrast is where the truth actually lies. The greater the accomplishment, the more you can be certain that they were surrounded by a powerful team. Individuals who accomplish great things never accomplish them alone. They were all the recipients of a gift. They were given the gift of visibility, while those who served tirelessly behind them embraced the path of anonymity. For every name that is known, there is an endless number of names that remain unknown, and the unknown were as essential to success and as vital to the achievements as those upon whom we place the mantle of greatness. Greatness is a gift given to individuals by those who choose to surround them with their own greatness. Let me repeat myself: no great endeavor has ever been accomplished alone.

Yet this realization does not diminish the greatness of the individuals we hold up as inspirations to us all. The fact that personal greatness is never achieved alone, the fact that personal greatness is always the sum total of the hard work and deep commitment of an untold number of people, does not in any way diminish the grandeur of an individual's accomplishments. In fact, it elevates it. It's much easier to do something yourself. It takes so much more work, it demands so much of yourself, to create an environment where highly talented, skilled, and intelligent people can work together for a common goal. If anything, this is the true genius behind all greatness. It is most certainly true when we are dealing with sustained greatness. What I've observed over the years is that all of us can have moments of greatness and glimpses of greatness, but what seems so unattainable is sustaining the level of commitment, resolve, and quality that achieves sustained greatness. That is why I am always fascinated by those who not only accomplish something extraordinary once but do it over and over again.

One of those extraordinary people I have had the privilege to come to know is Mark Burnett.

NO LONE SURVIVORS

I had just finished speaking at an event when someone came and told me that Mark Burnett wanted to say hello and asked if I had time to meet him. Honestly, the first thing that ran through my mind was, *It can't be* the *Mark Burnett.* After all, why in the world would *the* Mark Burnett be at all interested in saying hi to me? But I agreed just in case it was actually *the* Mark Burnett. And to my surprise, I was meeting one of the most extraordinary producers in television history. Mark Burnett is the genius behind *Survivor, The Apprentice, The Voice, Shark Tank,* and *500 Questions,* just to name a few of his groundbreaking and award-winning shows. If he had only one of these shows to his credit, his life would still be a case study of extraordinary success. But what most of us could not do once, he has done so many times over that he has made it look easy.

He is married to Roma Downey, who is best remembered for her angelic role in *Touched by an Angel*. Together they launched a record-setting series on the History Channel called *The Bible*. If you know anything about Mark and Roma, you know that they are a beautiful combination of boundless energy and extraordinary kindness. It shouldn't have come as a surprise to anyone that they would choose to take on the epic classic *Ben-Hur* and bring it back to the screen for a new generation to experience. I have never known anyone who lives out the adage "Go big or go home" in the way that Mark Burnett does. He is both tireless and fearless; he is driven and yet curiously exudes a deep love for life. You cannot be around Mark and not leave inspired and hopeful. He literally transmits courage to those around him.

I had the opportunity to ask Mark how he has been able to achieve the highest level of success in his industry not only once but repeatedly. He never mentioned any particular personal attribute or unique talent that he brought to the table. In fact, he never mentioned himself at all. His first response was to talk about his team. He explained that he has had the same team over the years and that it's that same team that he trusts with every great challenge he takes on.

To an outsider looking in, the answer seems obvious—it's all about Mark Burnett. He is unquestionably a creative genius who is fearless and undaunted by challenges. I personally still think all of that is true. But what we might miss in the light of the extraordinary nature of this man is that the singular competency that has allowed him to achieve success as if it is normative is that he has surrounded himself with a great team.

This is where most of us miss the boat. We've been misled to believe that if we have the potential for greatness in us, it means we don't need people to help us achieve that greatness. In fact, our sense of greatness might actually cause us to demean or diminish the value of other people. We think that life is either a sprint or a marathon but that in either case we are the only runner who matters. If life is a race, it is far more like a relay in which we do not win if we do not have a team that will help us get across the finish line.

On a personal level, Mark once said something to me that I will never forget. It was on one of those evenings when we had the privilege of visiting them in their home and sharing an amazing meal. As we were leaving, Mark and Roma walked us out to our car and casually offered us their place on the beach if we ever needed an escape or a haven to find some rest. I thanked them politely, but I had no intention of ever asking that of them. I think somehow he picked up on that particular nuance, because he reaffirmed the invitation, and then as I was turning to leave, he gently stopped me and said, "You need to believe in our friendship."

It's strange how words can affect us. I have thought about

those words from Mark many times since then. The statement went far deeper than any offer that he had graciously made to me. It made me wonder which friendships I believed in and which friendships I *could* believe in. It also made me ask myself, *Who are the people who can believe in my friendship?* Looking back, I realize that Mark's gracious words toward me were consistent with how he functioned in every arena of his life. Mark is all about people; he is about friendship. If there's one thing we should all learn from him, it is that if you are to achieve your greatest potential, if you are to live a life where you never settle, if you are going to strike the last arrow, you need to find your people. You need to at least be able to answer two questions: Who is with you? And who are you with?

THE EXPENDABLES

When we read Scripture, most often we are focused on what it says about God. We have been trained to be acutely aware of what we are to believe about God and how we are to relate to him. Yet Scripture is so much more than that. It gives us such keen insight into the human journey. From my vantage point, if we were to engage the Bible as a study in human sociology, the word that would emerge is *tribe*. The entire journey of Israel is about becoming a people. In fact, if the Scriptures are to be taken seriously, there is no journey toward God that does not bring us to each other.

You might begin the journey alone, but the place where God is taking you is a land called Together. If you have ever felt that you are living beneath your potential or that the greatness God has placed within you is yet to be realized, then I would tell you that the most common cause of living beneath our capacity is that we have chosen to walk alone rather than to walk together. You will never sustain greatness or fulfill your God-given calling if you see people as an obstacle to your destiny rather than as essential to fulfilling God's purpose in your life.

It's odd how we prioritize the things that matter to us. We choose a career or job; we choose a city or place to live. We make so many things important to us, but in all the things we factor in as we craft our futures, we make the people in our lives a commodity of, at best, secondary importance. We would take a job and give up our people rather than choose a tribe and give up the job. We don't say it like this, but many of us have been mentored by a culture that makes money more important than relationships. You can always meet new people; you can always make new friends; you can always find a new church. In our way of thinking, these are expendable, replaceable aspects of our lives. When it comes to relationships, many of us have chosen to be mercenaries.

The truth is, there *are* relationships that will keep you from the life God created you to live. There *are* people whom you need to extricate from your life because they pull you back to the person you were rather than forward to the person you must become. Yet this must never blind us to the deeper truth. We were not created to do life alone, and if we want people to be for us, then there need to be people whom we are for.

It is interesting that perhaps the most iconic shows that Mark Burnett brought to the screen are *Survivor* and *The Apprentice*. Both of those shows are about teaming, about learning to work together, about how if you are going to win as an individual, you need to learn how to win as a team. I have to wonder if these shows are simply external manifestations of Mark's internal world as a leader. There is an ancient African saying: "If you want to go fast, go alone. If you want to go far, go together." Mark has internalized that truth.

GOTRIBE

I have two friends whom I have journeyed with for over a decade now named Chris and Krickit Hodges. I knew them before they were married. I knew them before faith was a part of who they were. I met Chris when he was an atheist and was a trainer at 24-Hour Fitness. My wife and I became their friends while they were living together. We watched Chris go from an intellectual skeptic to a follower of Jesus. We watched Krickit as she rediscovered her faith. We married them in our backyard and followed them from health club to health club, both for our physical well-being and for their spiritual well-being.

Eventually they opened up their own club and named it

GoTRIBE in response to the language that I used in an earlier book called *The Barbarian Way*.[1] One of the chapters is titled "The Barbarian Tribe" and focuses on the power of being a people. Chris and Krickit adopted both the name and the philosophy of life. My wife began training with Krickit in hopes of winning a battle against weight that she felt was a losing struggle. For Kim, achieving physical health was deeply connected to her emotional well-being. My beautiful wife was an orphan from the age of eight to adulthood and at eight years old was left starving and abandoned in a government project. It's hard to understand the worries that set deeply into a child when she is uncertain if there will be enough food to eat and lives in fear of going hungry again. For Kim, this was a challenge that stood at the core of who she was as a person.

Krickit was exactly the person Kim needed. Kim not only began to lose a great deal of weight but also regained her natural athleticism. It was wonderful to see even her self-confidence elevating as she found success with her regimen at GoTRIBE. I began training at GoTRIBE only when Kim said she was going to quit. She felt bad that she was using our financial resources to secure a personal trainer. I felt the opposite. It was the best investment I could think of. She was more than worth the small amount of money that allowed her to have the context for success in an area of great challenge for her. So before I knew it, I was a member of GoTRIBE.

At first it wasn't as much a commitment to my own personal

health as it was wanting to be there to encourage Kim. After all, she was my people, and I needed to be there for her. After a few weeks, I started noticing how out of shape my staff was. Funny how you begin noticing that when you get in better shape. So I approached one of our pastors named Joe Smith. Joe was speaking more and was moving to a far more visible role at Mosaic. He's also one of the guys I would play basketball with all the time, and I needed him to regain his quickness. So I offered to sponsor Joe at GoTRIBE for the summer. He gladly accepted. And then I added a few others on our staff, giving them the opportunity to join GoTRIBE at my expense. Then it got out of hand and we decided to make this part of our health program for every employee and family member at Mosaic.

In less than a year, twenty people who had participated, including those on staff and their spouses who opted in, had lost a combined total of 177.8 pounds, losing 191 percent body fat, averaging 15 pounds of fat lost for each individual involved, not to mention the total of 268 inches lost across the board. And it was the women who proved to be the athletic beasts in our tribe. Some of our guys required a little bit of shame and prodding to not allow their wives to leave them in the dust. Everyone, though, has expressed how moving together toward health has radically changed their lives and even dramatically affected the sense of camaraderie and closeness of our team. On a surface level, everyone looks better, but underneath the surface, this journey has strangely made us more tight knit. We were already a pretty tight crew.

This commitment to each other's health and well-being has made us far more of a family than a staff.

I mentioned the African saying when talking about Mark Burnett because Chris and Krickit have a variation of it on their wall. But after seeing so much transformation take place for our team and so much success for individuals who throughout their lives had known only frustration and failure when it came to their own health challenges, I sent Chris and Krickit this quote instead: "If you want to go fast, go alone; if you want to go far, go together; if you want to go far fast, GoTRIBE."

I assure you this is true in every arena of life. You will go faster and farther when you find your tribe. When you find a people committed to a common mission, a common purpose, you find those individuals who are like hearted and like minded and carry the same fire you carry and whose passion burns as brightly as yours. People don't slow you down; the *wrong* people slow you down. When you choose the right people, when you find your people, your life begins to come together in a way that it never could when you walk alone.

CLOSER THAN A BROTHER

If we are not careful, we will spend our entire lives trying to find ourselves and never realize that we never fully become ourselves until we find our people. Perhaps no one has popularized the idea of finding "your person" more than Shonda Rhimes has through her characters on *Grey's Anatomy*. We all long for that one person who gets us, that person who we know is always for us, that person who we are always for.

It's fascinating to me that the concept that popularized *Grey's Anatomy* is actually profoundly expressed in the ancient book of Kings. David and Jonathan had the kind of relationship that often is translated only to contemporary culture. Jonathan was the son of King Saul. In any other scenario, Jonathan would be understood to be the rightful heir to the crown. It was his birthright and his bloodline, yet David was the one whom God would choose to be king. It wasn't something David sought after nor something he asked for. He was plucked out of obscurity and selected by God to replace Saul and become the king of Israel. This should have made David and Jonathan the greatest of enemies. It's the material from which generations of conflict are created.

In a strange and unexpected turn of events, David goes to Jonathan and tells him that King Saul intends him harm and, in fact, intends to end David's life.[2] Jonathan assures David this cannot possibly be true, but that if it is true, he will use his relationship to his father to secure that information and protect David. The extraordinary nature of this relationship cannot be overstated: a man who would value a friendship more than his own success. For Jonathan, the question of who should be king is never in question. It is clear to him that David is the one God has chosen. It takes an incredible strength of character to be willing to give up something that should have been yours and recognize there is another who is better suited for the task. Jonathan's allegiance to David is unequivocal. "Whatever you want me to do," he says, "I'll do for you."³ Jonathan was declaring to David, *I am with you.*

Long before David was king, he had found his person—the one who was closer than a brother. Jonathan was committed to the greatness of David even at the cost of his own fame and future. But the commitment wasn't one sided. This allegiance went both ways. We are told later that "Jonathan had David reaffirm his oath out of love for him, because he loved him as he loved himself."⁴ Though David was one of many brothers, it was Jonathan who became closer than a brother.

Over the days and months to come, David would be joined by a legion of the greatest soldiers who walked the earth in those days.⁵ From Shammah, who stood in the field of lentils and fought the Philistines, to Eleazar, who fought in battle until the sword froze to his hand, to Josheb-Basshebeth, who raised his spear against eight hundred men in one encounter and defeated them all. There were three unnamed warriors who heard David long for water from a well near Bethlehem, and without being asked or instructed, they crossed enemy lines to refresh their leader's thirst. Of course there is Benaiah, who killed a lion in a pit on a snowy day—because it would have been easy if it had not been snowing. There were leaders of hundreds and leaders of thousands. There was an inner circle of thirty who were David's most trusted warriors. And we are told there were the three—the three who stood at his side who loved David more than their very own lives and who David trusted with his very own life.

The story of Israel is wrapped up in the kingdom that David established, but there has never existed a kingdom that David established alone. What we remember is a young shepherd boy named David who went face to face against Goliath with a sling and a stone and killed the warrior giant. We remember David as the giant killer and then misattribute all of his success and all of his conquests to him alone. David killed the giant and earned the trust of those who cowered before the ominous figure, but the future that God was calling him into could not be fulfilled if he had walked into every battle alone. To fulfill his destiny, he would need to find his band of brothers.

YOUR FUTURE IS IN PEOPLE

In a completely different context, we find the same principle in the lives of three widows who found themselves alone in the world after famine and misfortune had taken the lives of everyone they loved and who loved them. We are told that in the days when judges ruled, there was a famine so severe that it left these three women—Naomi, Orpah, and Ruth—without fathers, without husbands, and without sons. Naomi instructed her two daughters-in-law to go back to their own people and make a new life for themselves. She saw no future or hope for herself and felt that the best hope for the only family she had left was for them to go back to the families they had left. She had no ill will against them, but for them to stay with her now would be unreasonable. In the midst of this moment, they all began to weep and wailed out loud in their sorrow.

Little is known about the future of Orpah. She kissed Naomi good-bye and went to find her people, who she calculated quite reasonably would be her only hope for her future. In returning to them, she did nothing wrong.

Ruth made a different decision. Ruth was a Moabite. She had a people she could return to and look to for help, but she refused to leave Naomi. She understood there was something more powerful than blood, a connection more important than where a person came from. She spoke those words that will be echoed for the rest of human history: "Where you go I will go, and where you stay I will stay. Your people will be my people and your God my God."[6]

It is from here that the book of Ruth is written. It is because of this decision that Ruth's story demands to be told. Orpah chose a future that she might find in the people who were once hers. Ruth made a new group of people her future. She had no promise of a future and a hope. If anything, she expected that she and Naomi would die together. For Ruth it was simple: "Where you die I will die, and there I will be buried. May the LORD deal with me, be it ever so severely, if even death separates you and me."[7]

The story of Ruth unfolds like a romance novel. She works as a servant girl in the field, and the owner of that field, whose name is

Boaz, sees her and is drawn to her beauty. But when he realizes there is more in her than meets the eye and falls in love with her, he recalls that there is another man who holds a position of responsibility to the household of Naomi and that it is both this man's obligation and his right to claim Ruth as his own wife. Boaz cleverly convinces him that he doesn't want the burden of having to care for Ruth the rest of her life, and so the other man relinquishes his position to Boaz. In this way, Boaz claims the role of what is known as the guardian redeemer, and Ruth becomes the wife of one of the most prominent and wealthy men among his people.

Boaz, we are then told, was the father of Obed, and Obed was the father of Jesse, and Jesse was the father of David. David, of course, would become king, and it's from his lineage that the Messiah would come. And so this woman Ruth, who chooses her people and decides that their future will be her future as well, becomes one of the four women mentioned in the lineage of Jesus of Nazareth.

So often, when we think about the will of God or we're frantically trying to discern what God wants to do with our lives, we evaluate opportunities and never fully consider relationships. Who are the people you have bound your life to? Who are the people in your life to whom you have declared, "I am with you"? The future that God wants for you will never come at the expense of the people he brings into your life. That doesn't mean you don't lose people along the way. It doesn't mean there aren't people you have to leave behind. It does mean you don't live for yourself and yourself alone.

Whatever you do, you need to find your tribe. If you are a zebra, find the zebras and run with them. If you are a gazelle, then find the herd that runs at your pace. If you are a lion, find your pride. Finding your tribe is not about being of the same color or same ethnicity or same history; it's about being of one heart and mind. So whatever you do, whatever it takes, wherever you need to go, whatever you need to do, find your tribe and begin to walk together. Your best future is waiting in your deepest relationships.

ROMEO AND JULIET

Brian Larrabee is one of those people you never forget once you've met him—six foot five inches, big personality, with a passionate desire to make the world a better place. He's the founder of Good City Mentors, and for as long as I have known him, he's been pouring his life into young men who lacked the opportunity to have strong male figures in their lives. In 2015 he was recruited to serve on a team going to Shanghai, China. This team was led by David Arcos, who has been the pastor of creative arts at Mosaic for the past twenty years. There is an unusual phenomenon in China where the children of educated Chinese businesspeople, feeling crushed under the weight of expectation, have been a part of an escalation of depression and suicides. Our team in Los Angeles was bringing together a troupe of creative artists who would go and invest in these young students, both to inspire their creative imagination and to infuse hope into their lives.

Brian joined David's team early, but as life would have it, his obligations in Los Angeles began to press him, and he asked David if he could withdraw from his commitment. His nonprofit had just secured funding, and now it didn't make sense for him to travel across the world to do good when he could do good at home. David was not inclined to let Brian off the hook easily. He told him that he had made a commitment and should keep it, that he had a pattern of backing out of things, and that if he kept this commitment, it would cause his donors to trust him even more. David went as far as to tell Brian that he felt certain that if he would keep this commitment, God would bless him in ways he would never imagine.

I feel strongly that a significant element to Brian's distress was having a personal relationship in his life come to an end. The person who mattered deeply to him had just ended their relationship, and we all know how heartbreak can leave us debilitated. One of the hardest things to convince people of is that when you have lost a person, you should find your people. Brian made the decision to keep his commitment and go to China, but even more than that, he made a decision to trust God with his future.

Also on this team was one of America's premier ballerinas. Allyssa Bross is the face of the Los Angeles Ballet. Her résumé spans from *Swan Lake* to *Romeo and Juliet* to *The Nutcracker*. Allyssa was sixteen years old when she was accepted into the

School of American Ballet, and after only two years, she signed a contract with the Los Angeles Ballet. Within her first year in LA and before she was even twenty years old, she was promoted to the company's first ever principal dancer. She had been part of Mosaic for nearly two years and had heard about the opportunity to go serve in Shanghai. Her involvement came about in an unusual way.

While sitting at a table with Allyssa at a fund-raising event for the ballet company, some donors heard about her desire to go to China and were so moved by her story that they as a table funded her entire trip. This created a huge concern for the ballet company, as the donors had been brought there to support the Los Angeles Ballet, not Allyssa. But they quickly realized that it was in no way competition with their ambitions. Allyssa was completely committed to both the ballet and going to serve in China.

It's kind of a far-fetched story that two people who both go to the same church and live in the same city would have to be on a team going to Shanghai, China, to actually meet for the first time. Yet it was while they were in Shanghai, not thinking of themselves but completely giving themselves to serving others, that they found each other. Neither Brian nor Allyssa could have ever guessed that choosing to be part of this tribe, choosing to join on this particular mission, would result in finding the perfect person to marry.

So many people desperately search for their person, when what they need to do is search for their people. It is a beautiful thing to watch when two people don't even know they are searching for each other but find each other when they are pursuing their purpose and have committed themselves to a people. Ruth never could have seen that Boaz was waiting on the other side of Naomi. David never could have predicted that it would be Jonathan who would stand between him and King Saul.

Years ago, when I spent a great deal of my time trying to understand successful patterns in business, I began to discover that often the initial idea of entrepreneurs is not their best idea, but what happens in that first endeavor is that they find their best people. They find the people who are with them whether the idea pans out or not. They find the people who are with them both in the midst of success and in the midst of failure.

Your ideas will change, your challenges will change, the world will change, but when you know who is with you and you know who you are with, you can face whatever is yet to come.

THE BEST OF THE BEST

Anyone who knows me knows I love basketball. Last year I grabbed my son, Aaron, and a friend and took them to game one of the NBA Finals between the Warriors and the Cavaliers. It was electric to be in Oracle Arena watching two of the greatest players in the world compete against each other. We didn't know who would win, but if there was one thing we all thought was certain, it was that either Steph Curry or LeBron James would be the

MVP. Both teams had great players, but they were the supporting cast. In the end, it would come down to the stars. It would be either LeBron or Steph, and the series would not only decide a champion but would answer the question once and for all who the greatest player in the world really was.

Six games later, the Warriors defeated the Cavs four games to two, and the 2015 MVP, of course, was Andre Iguodala. Don't feel bad if you do not recognize that name. I'm not even sure that people who follow basketball would recognize the name. Andre Iguodala wasn't even a starter in 2015. Coach Steven Kerr asked him to come off the bench and play the role of the sixth man. Every team has five players who are designated as starters, and every team works to build a strong bench that can step in when the starters need to step off the court. But perhaps the most significant player on the team, the one who can push the team into the status of greatness, is what is known as the sixth man. He is the singular player that could be a starter anywhere but chooses to come off the bench to make the team stronger. It would not be an understatement to say that Iguodala was not happy with the opportunity. He jokingly stated that if he was going to come off the bench, it had better be worth it in terms of results. As it worked out, Andre Iguodala was entrusted with the nearly impossible task of covering LeBron James. And though he would have been listed as the sixth most important player on the Warriors' roster, when all was said and done, he was awarded the most valuable player of the NBA Finals.

If we were all to be perfectly honest, when we dream about our lives, we think of ourselves as one day hopefully being either like LeBron James or Steph Curry, or someone comparable to them in another arena of life. Rarely do we imagine ourselves as the guy sitting on the bench when the game starts or the person who somehow loses his job to someone he would consider a lesser player. The tragedy in life is that far too many of us would rather be the star on a losing team than the complementary player on the championship team. But those who have followed sports over the decades have seen a peculiar pattern when it comes to great athletes. They play on a great team; they increase their personal value; they choose to leave that team for a lesser team that will pay them more; then they never again achieve the level of success they knew in the past. Great teams make average players good and good players great.

When you surround yourself with great people, it elevates who you are. If you want to have great character, surround yourself with people of great character. If you want to take great risks, surround yourself with a tribe of risk takers. If you want to live a life of adventure, then choose a tribe that makes life an adventure. You will become who you walk with. So imagine the implications if you decide to walk with Jesus. When he calls you, he never calls you to only yourself. He always calls you to a people. He always calls us to each other.

So the questions remain, who are you with? Who have you given yourself to? Who are you willing to stand shoulder to shoulder with, come hell or high water, and who is with you? Who can you trust? Who's got your back? Who will pick you up when you fall?

In Ecclesiastes, Solomon reminds us of how important it is to never walk alone:

> Two are better than one,
>> because they have a good return for their labor:
> If either of them falls down,
>> one can help the other up.
> But pity anyone who falls
>> and has no one to help them up.
> Also, if two lie down together, they will keep warm.
>> But how can one keep warm alone?
> Though one may be overpowered,
>> two can defend themselves.
> A cord of three strands is not quickly broken.[8]

When my family and I were traveling in South Africa, we had the opportunity to go on a safari. So we went out into the Serengeti and had this extraordinary experience together. We spent the night in the middle of the jungle, and we were supposed to wait until the morning before we went exploring to see if we could find any of the wild animals—any of the big five. But most of us were too impatient to wait until the morning. One of our guides grabbed us—or we grabbed him—and we went out in an open

Jeep. Five of us jumped in to go exploring in the middle of the night.

So the guide, my wife and I, and our son and daughter went exploring in the wilds of Africa. We didn't really know if we would find anything, but as we were driving in the pitch dark of night, we realized we were suddenly surrounded by a pride of lions— four or five of these giant beasts just walking within touching distance of our vehicle. It was one of the most extraordinary and beautiful experiences I've ever had in my life. It's one thing to see a lion in an unnatural setting in the zoo, but it's another to see that beautiful creature in all its power and glory in the wild.

In that moment, I thought about the fact that we didn't have any doors, didn't have a roof, and were clearly exposed. If these lions were hungry, they could easily have attacked us, and our tour would be over. Our guide instructed us—very, very quietly—not to make any sudden movements, not to speak loudly, not to get out of the vehicle. He said, "If you get out of the vehicle, the lions will most likely attack you. The key is staying together and staying together inside of this Jeep. Because when the lions look at us, they will see us as one creature, not five unprotected humans." When we stood together, when we journeyed together, we had a strength and a fearsomeness in the minds of the lions that we would not have had if we were standing alone.

This principle held true in the jungles of Africa, and it holds true in the jungles of Los Angeles. In fact, this is a principle that will hold true for all of us at any time in our lives: we are more powerful when we walk together, and we are more vulnerable when we walk alone.

It's essential—above everything else you pursue in life, whatever else you may desire or long for, whether it's success or wealth or power or celebrity—to make sure that nothing in your life has a greater value than finding your tribe. You need to find your people, because as long as you walk alone, you will never know your strength. Your greatest strength is not when you can prove that you don't need anyone; your greatest strength is when you no longer have to prove that you can do it alone. There is strength in numbers. There is a strength that comes when you walk together with those who are of one heart and one mind as you.

To live the life God created you to live, to ensure that everything within you is unleashed for the good of humanity, even if your ultimate longing is to find yourself, you need to find your people.

KNOW WHAT YOU WANT

I wonder where the tradition of asking children what they want to do when they grow up began. After all, it's a strange thought that an eight-year-old would have any realistic idea of what he or she wants to do in life. Maybe we're trying to ask them before they turn eighteen, when we know they will have no idea. But wherever the tradition began, it says more about us that we ask it than whatever it tells us about the child. I imagine it's more for self-amusement, as children will say the funniest things. I don't think we really expect them to know what they want to do later in life.

Wouldn't it be great if all of us from our earliest years in life had absolute clarity about the direction of our lives? For most of us, we got it wrong when we were eight, we got it wrong when we were eighteen, we're pretty sure we got it wrong at twenty-eight, and at thirty-eight we start feeling an overwhelming sense of despair that the life we have is not the one we wanted. It's usually not that we changed our minds about what we wanted; it's that we didn't know what we wanted. For far too many of us, we end up feeling as if our lives just happened rather than that our lives were what we chose to happen.

There are those rare individuals who are so talented from a young age that their talent demands their lives. I don't know if Mozart had much of a choice about what he would do in life, or Monet. Tiger Woods was swinging a club at four years old. Michael Jordan was clearly not born for baseball. When you are ten years old and you're Bobby Fischer, you're going to play chess. You know what you want because it wanted you.

For the rest of us who are not burdened by such an extraordinary talent that it demands our lives, we are often left more as if we're walking in a fog. Everyone around us will have an idea of what we should do—*pursue your dreams, follow your passions, develop some skills.* But in the end, those ideas are more about the resources we apply to our lives and less about the lives we want to give ourselves to.

I am always amazed when I meet someone who knows exactly what he or she wants. It gives a person such a sense of clarity and conviction. I've also journeyed with people who were sure they knew what they wanted, and it never happened for them. Those are the times when people feel so disoriented and uncertain, not only about their future but about themselves too.

I fall into the category of those who had no idea what they were going to do when they grew up. Even in the small things, I lacked the necessary certainty to succeed. I grew up loving basketball, but I played football and ran track. My stepdad loved football, and track was its complement during the off-season. It wasn't that I didn't love football; it's just that most people born in Latin America are not physically designed for American football. It would have been wiser for me to follow the steps of the soccer player Lionel Messi or the basketball star Chris Paul than to try to be like the football standouts Lawrence Taylor and Curtis Martin.

When we moved from Miami to North Carolina, my brother and I were the new recruits for the high school football team. The coach asked Alex what position he played, and he said, "Quarterback." When the coach asked me, I had no idea how to answer. My best position would have been quarterback, but my brother was already a great quarterback, and I was not his equal. So I thought my answer should be broader. When the coach asked me, "What position do you play?" I said, "I play football." He loved the answer. I hated the result. The truth is, I had no idea what my position on a football team was, nor did I have any idea what my position in life was.

What I learned from twenty years of indecisiveness is that you will either define yourself or be defined by others. You will either choose your life or live a life that was never meant to be yours. How you end is profoundly affected by how you begin. You never begin the journey of creating the life you want until you know what you want. It's only when you know what you want that you can say no to everything that wants you. I've seen it over and over again. You will never get what you want until you know what you want.

WHEN I GROW UP I WANT . . .

I met Jimmy and Sis Blanchard at a leadership conference in Florida where I was a speaker. Retired by then, Jimmy had formerly served as the chairman and CEO of Synovus, a multibillion-dollar financial services company based in Columbus, Georgia. He believes that one of the greatest gifts he can offer this country is an investment in leadership. That's why he speaks at events with some of the biggest-name speakers and runs the Jim Blanchard Leadership Forum.[1] Yet he is also one of the most humble and unassuming men you will ever meet. When you sit with Jimmy, you would have no idea how much he has accomplished, but you would not be able to escape his deep affection for his wife and family.

I'll never forget the one story that gave me the greatest insight into the man he has become and the journey it took to get him there. Too often we project that all successful people began with a sense of clarity and certainty, but Jimmy reminds us that knowing what we want often comes in a crisis of uncertainty. Because he didn't know what he wanted, he almost lost the life God wanted for him. This is a cautionary tale that fortunately turned into a great love story. And if you feel it's too late for you to reclaim your life, here is a reminder that it's never too late—or at least better late than never. It was all about how he got Sis to marry him.

I wish this were a story of love at first sight, but it's not. I would even be willing to accept a story about a man who passionately pursued the woman of his dreams until she finally relented, but it's not. The reason this story has so much power is that it is both real life and a metaphor for how easy it is to miss out on what is right in front of us. So often we desperately want God to give us what we want, and we feel frustrated that he doesn't seem to come through. Yet the reality is that far too often God puts right in front of us what our hearts have longed for, but we don't have the eyes to see it. In the most tragic of cases, we wait too long, we make too many mistakes, we give up on the search, we sadly conclude that we have missed our moments. Regardless of how long it takes us to know what it is we want with all our hearts, the moment we know it, we need to go for it.

It all began in the fall of 1961, when Sis was a sophomore at the University of Georgia. She was invited to a brunch and asked to bring a date. A friend got her a date with a student named Jimmy Blanchard. Like I said, it wasn't love at first sight. Still, they hit it off well enough that the next week, Jimmy called Sis and asked her to go to the Georgia/Florida football game. They drove to it together and had a great time. They began to date, and Sis hoped it would lead to something more.

Then one night in May of 1962, Jimmy asked Sis out and drove her to a parking lot and turned off the car. He turned to her and said, "I think our relationship has reached a point where we need to either get more serious or stop dating." Sis was about to say, "Let's get more serious," when he said, "I think we should stop dating." So that was the end of the relationship . . . for the time being.

They hardly saw each other at all for the next couple years.

Jimmy went to law school. Sis graduated from college and moved back home. She assumed Jimmy had forgotten her, and although he had expected to forget her, memories of Sis kept coming back to his mind.

So one night in the summer of 1964, Jimmy called Sis out of the blue. He asked her if they could have dinner. She eagerly said yes and hoped it would be the rekindling of a relationship that hadn't developed as she had hoped. But after that one evening, he was no surer about the relationship than he had been before, so he went silent on her again.

By the fall of 1964, Sis had moved on. She met a wonderful young man we will call Sam. A few months later, they were engaged to be married. Jimmy was a thing of the past, a memory of something that was seemingly never meant to be.

Jimmy, in the meantime, was due to graduate from law school the following spring and report to the army in June for a two-year commitment. It was on a Saturday, playing golf with his dad, when Jimmy confessed that he had hoped that he and Sis would have worked things out. His dad asked if she knew how he felt about her, and Jimmy said no. Then his dad gave him some wise advice: "I don't think I'd let the sun go down without getting her on the phone."

So Jimmy did just that. He called Sis, and her mother answered the phone. He asked her if she knew if Sis had plans for the next Sunday night. Sis's mother responded, "Oh, Jimmy, you haven't heard! Sis is engaged."

Jimmy was stunned—but not thwarted. The next evening, he called Sis and asked if he could see her. Assuming he was just coming as an old friend, she said that would be fine. (I do think it's interesting to note that she never mentioned it to Sam.)

When Jimmy arrived, Sis promptly showed him her ring. Then, at Jimmy's request, they went to his car to talk. As soon as they'd shut the cars doors, Jimmy turned to her and said, "I didn't come here to congratulate you but to talk you out of your engagement because I want you to marry me and be the mother of my children." Sis was amazed by this. They talked until two in the morning. Their conversation was finally interrupted when her father walked over and asked what was going on. Jimmy responded that they were just talking, and he quickly left.

After that night, Jimmy didn't call Sis again. She decided not to break off her engagement and to marry Sam and put Jimmy behind her. So she went on with her life, had her wedding parties, picked out her china, and prepared herself for a life with Sam.

Jimmy, meanwhile, went off to Fort Benjamin Harrison in Indianapolis for finance school and began a two-year military commitment. From there he wrote Sis a letter, saying he understood that this was the way it was going to be and he wished her well and happiness. This last letter was so unlike Jimmy. Sis had never known him to back down or surrender. She was always drawn to his raw courage. Perhaps it was only out of respect for Sis and Sam that Jimmy pulled back.

Now their future was in Sis's hands. As she came closer to her wedding day, she grew undeniably unhappy. She knew that even though she loved Sam, she was not in love with him. And even though she had no promise that Jimmy would ever return, she knew that she could not marry Sam if she could not give him all of her heart. When she told her parents, they were filled with relief, letting Sis know that they had never felt that the two were right for each other.

As every great love story finds its way to an unexpected reunion—that moment when two people who have wandered away from each other find that the universe has somehow brought them back together—Sis unexpectedly received a phone call from Jimmy inviting her to join him at the wedding of mutual friends. He suggested that after the wedding she go with him and his parents to the beach at Alligator Point for the Fourth of July. Sis eagerly said yes.

After the wedding, when they were walking on the beach, Jimmy knew that he could not wait any longer. He expressed to Sis that he still wanted to marry her. Sis had assured her father that even though she was going to spend a few days with Jimmy, she would not be impulsive in any way. Yet when Jimmy asked her if she would marry him, without hesitation she said yes. So much for not being impulsive!

On December 18, 1965, Jimmy and Sis were married. It was a small wedding in comparison to the one that had been canceled earlier that year, but what they lacked in the grandeur of a wedding, they gained in knowing that they were each marrying the love of their life.

I tell you this story for one specific reason. Although it took quite a while, there was a clear shift in Jimmy's approach towards life—we see it in his change of heart towards Sis. He could have missed his one true love by not knowing what he wanted. Indecision is not a decision.

We often wonder what it is that separates those who achieve great things from those who only long to do something significant with their lives. What I've seen in Jimmy transcends every area of his life. It has shaped his life of faith, it has shaped his business success, and as we've journeyed through his romance, we've seen that it definitely shaped his marriage. Jimmy refused to let circumstances or even propriety stop him from getting what he wanted. Sis was the love of his life, and he would not settle for anyone else.

To live a life in which you strike your last arrow, where you never settle for less, you have to know what you want. And when you know what you want, you have to muster up the courage and faith to pursue it with all your might. It would have been so easy for Jimmy to give up on ever winning Sis's heart since she was committed to another man. And believe me, I'm not encouraging anyone to interfere in someone else's marriage plans. But isn't this the stuff of every classic love story—not settling for less, not choosing to marry the person whom you do not love only because you do not believe the one you love can ever be yours? This is one of the attributes of Jimmy Blanchard that I like the most: he doesn't stop until he has a clear sense of what he is to accomplish in life, and he pursues that intention fearlessly.

So often you blame God for the life you have, but you do not know what life you want. Certainly there is a dilemma here. The life you want may not be the life God wants for you. This is why the process must begin by loving God first. It is in loving God with all your heart and mind and soul that he begins to shape your passions. When God has your heart, you can trust your desires. His will is not a map; it is a match. He shows you the way by setting you on fire. You will know God's desire for you by the fire in you! The fire in you will light the way.

WHEN GOD ASKS A QUESTION

There is a story in the life of Jesus that has always struck me as odd. It's about a time when Jesus was leaving Jericho and a large crowd began to follow him. In the midst of all that chaos and commotion, two blind men were sitting by the road.

> When they heard that Jesus was going by, they shouted, "Lord, son of David, have mercy on us!"
>
> The crowd rebuked them and told them to be quiet, but they shouted all the louder, "Lord, Son of David, have mercy on us!"
>
> Jesus stopped and called them. "What do you want me to do for you?" he asked.[2]

That has to be the most unnecessary question I have ever heard. I mean, I say this with all respect. But have you ever been asked a question with such an obvious answer? Like when someone calls you in the middle of the night and the first thing he says is, "Did I wake you?" Of course he woke you! It's four o'clock in the morning. I think next time I'll simply respond, "No, I was sitting by the phone waiting for you to call."

But the two blind men answered Jesus's question by saying, "Lord, . . . we want our sight." Then "Jesus had compassion on them and touched their eyes. Immediately they received their sight and followed him."[3]

Usually when we read a story like this, we are struck by the outcome. It's no small thing that two blind men received their sight. It's incredibly hopeful and heartwarming that Jesus had compassion on them and also had the power to heal. So the question he had asked them often goes overlooked. After all, if Jesus is God, he would already know the answer to it. But even if he wasn't God, I think he probably could have picked up on the clues. Two blind men desperately crying out for help, "Have mercy on us!"

"What do you want me to do for you?"

I thought through the options. "Jesus, I heard you were a carpenter. Could you make me a really nice cane? That way I can use it to stumble my way through life." Or "Could you, Jesus, in your great generosity, get us a Roman chariot? With driver provided, since we're blind?"

When Jesus asked the men, "What do you want me to do for

you?" it wasn't because Jesus didn't know but because he needed them to declare what they wanted him to do on their behalf.

"We want our sight."

I wonder how many times God has asked us, "What do you want me to do for you?" and in false humility we stammered and said, "Whatever you want to do, Lord, is fine."

The psalmist David tells us that we are to delight ourselves in the Lord and he will give us the desires of our heart.[4] This means we need to know our hearts, we need to know our desires, and we must allow those desires to first be informed and then formed by our love and worship of God. He shapes his will in us far more than he speaks his will to us. If we want to know what God wants, we need to give him our hearts and let him build desires in us that we want more than anything else in the world. That is why the asking is so important.

If you don't know what you want, then God's trying to give you what he wants for you is a wasted effort. You have to want what God wants in order to receive what he wants to give you. Jesus fully intended to give sight to these two men who were blind, but imagine if, when he asked that question, they had asked him for so much less than he longed to provide for them. I'm convinced there are many of us who are walking blind because we ask God for a cane rather than for sight. It is clear that there are times in life when it is not within the scope of God's intention for our life to give us certain things we ask for. But wouldn't you rather err by asking for too much than too little?

The truth is that many of us ask very little of God because we think very little of him. We are afraid to pray big prayers because if God doesn't come through, it might shatter our faith. I'm convinced that far too often we try to protect God with our prayers. We ask him to do only what we can do ourselves so that we don't put him in an embarrassing predicament and prove to unbelievers that God is not nearly as powerful as we had hoped. I can assure you that God does not need our protection. He doesn't need our small prayers to protect his big name. Is it possible that our dreams are too small for God and that our ambitions are too small to need God? If we choose to live a small life, we do not make enough room for a big God. Over and over again in the Scriptures, God calls men and women who think very little of themselves to accomplish great things. God takes men and women who felt too small for a big life and challenged them to dream big and to live big.

WHEN IT'S TIME TO GO BIG

It was the week before Easter in 1981. I was a senior at the University of North Carolina, Chapel Hill. At that time, my life of organized sports had come to an end, but I was still an avid and passionate athlete and always found a way to compete. I was playing in a soccer league when an opposing player clipped my leg and damaged my knee. I was in so much pain that night that I could barely sleep. My college roommate had built a loft where we could sleep, giving us more floor space to live. During that night,

I kept tossing back and forth. It seemed every time I was almost comfortable, the position of my leg sent pain running through my body. Sometime in the middle of the night, I rolled too far, fell out of the loft, and landed with severe force on top of my roommate's army surplus locker. When I landed, my elbow was trapped between my body and the corner of that locker, and I could tell something had broken.

A few minutes after I fell, while I lay there moaning and unable to get a word out of my mouth, I heard my roommate ask, "Did you drop something, or was that you?"

After he realized that it was me lying on the floor, I asked him if he would get me to the hospital. I would have thought it was my good fortune that my roommate majored in physical therapy, but it was not to be. He decided to leave me there all night on the floor and assured me he would help me get to the hospital in the morning. It was a rough night. In the morning, I got myself to the hospital, and after quite a few X-rays, the doctors explained to me that the radial head on my elbow had been broken and that there was high likelihood I would not regain the movement in my arm. Did I mention that my arm was frozen at a thirty-degree angle? I began physical therapy at the University of North Carolina Medical Center, and my range of motion was zero, zero, zero, zero. I was twenty-two years old and a new follower of Christ.

I was a musician who was performing in festivals and events and trying to do it all to connect people to the God whom I had just recently met. At last my life seemed to be going in the right direction. I know I wasn't getting it all right, but I was living with a passion and intensity that I felt certain was what God wanted from me, and then this had to go and happen. It came as a significant betrayal. Why did God let this happen to me? The idea that I would never move my arm again was a paralyzing thought.

That same week, I received a phone call from an organization coming from Canada to North Carolina. They were putting on a large festival and somehow had gotten my name and asked if I could perform at it. I didn't want to tell them I had just broken my elbow and had been informed that I would never use my arm again. For some unexplainable reason, I simply said, "Count me in."

I sat down after finishing the phone call, put my guitar on my lap, and began to pray. I didn't want to ask God for too much. That seemed to smack of arrogance. And the last thing I wanted to express to God was a sense of entitlement. So I prayed a very simple prayer, a very specific prayer, a very small prayer: "God, would you move my arm to the strings of the guitar so that I could at least play in the festival?" I wasn't asking for much, just a fifteen-degree adjustment on my paralyzed arm.

If you are a person who believes in healing, then what happened next is perfectly understandable. If you don't believe that God heals people in the world today, you might find the next thing I tell you to be incredible. All I can tell you is that in that moment, my arm instantly moved to the exact place where the strings of my guitar sat. For me being new to faith, this was an amazing miracle. The moment I prayed, God said yes and moved my arm. It was as if Jesus looked at me and said, "What do you want me to do for you?" And I said, "I know what I want. I want my arm to be stuck exactly where I can play the strings of the guitar for the rest of my life."

It was in that moment that I realized how stupid my prayer was. I mean, it's one thing not to believe that God will heal you. If you do not believe that God heals, then it makes perfect sense not to pray for healing. But I actually believed that God could heal me and was certain God not only has the power to heal but often has the intention to heal. The moment I saw my arm move, I realized that was the stupidest prayer I could have ever prayed. After all, if God would answer that prayer, he would have answered a bigger prayer. If he immediately moved my arm to where I asked, why wouldn't he completely heal my arm if I had asked for that? When Jesus asked me, "What do you want?" I said, "I know what I want—I want the cane," without realizing he really wanted to give me my sight. I wonder how many of us choose our paralysis and then blame God for never telling us to rise and walk.

That was Good Friday of 1981. By Monday, I returned to physical therapy at the UNC Medical Center. When they graphed my progress, I had moved from zero, zero, zero, zero to complete recovery, with no medical explanation for my healing. That first movement came instantly, but the rest of my ability came over a weekend of hard work. It was not without pain; it was not without struggle. To this day I feel the effects of that break. After all, in this life all healing is temporary. Perhaps what God was trying to teach me was that he can heal. I think what he was trying to put into me is that what would change my life the most powerfully would be to stop settling for less.

When you go to God, go big, dream big, pray big, ask big, live big. You will never live so big that you are too big for God. If you don't know what you want, you will get what you do not want. If you don't know who you want to become, you will become someone you never wanted to be. If you don't know what life you want to live, you're going to live the life someone else wants you to live. If you don't know what you want God to do in your life, you will wonder why he gave you so little, while the whole time he was waiting for you to see how much he wanted to entrust with you.

Remember, Elisha called the king out for not striking his last arrow. Elisha clearly had a mind-set of the abundance of God. He also knew that God would allow us to settle for less if we did not ask for the more.

WHEN ENOUGH ISN'T ENOUGH

A woman comes to Elisha. She is the widow of one of the prophets who served in Elisha's company. She goes to him when she is at the end of herself. She tells him, "Your servant my husband is dead, and you know that he revered the LORD. But now his creditor is coming to take my two boys as his slaves."[5]

Have you ever been in that place in your life where you feel like you have given God everything you have and yet feel that somehow God has abandoned you? Can you imagine living your life completely for the purpose of God and being completely abandoned, with no future or hope? This woman's circumstance could not be more tragic or unbearable. But to her credit, instead of turning from God, she turns to him by going to Elisha.

After hearing her situation, Elisha asks her a question that echoes the words of Jesus to the two blind men. "How can I help you?" In moments like those, you need to know what you want. Elisha presses in and asks her, "Tell me, what do you have in your house?"

Her response is a description of the state of her soul more than a description of her finances. She says, "Your servant has nothing there at all." And upon reflection she adds, "Except a small jar of olive oil."[6]

Elisha said, "Go around and ask all your neighbors for empty jars. Don't ask for just a few. Then go inside and shut the door behind you and your sons. Pour oil into all the jars, and as each is filled, put it to one side."

She left him and shut the door behind her and her sons. They brought the jars to her and she kept pouring. When all the jars were full, she said to her son, "Bring me another one."

But he replied, "There is not a jar left." Then the oil stopped flowing.

She went and told the man of God, and he said,
"Go, sell the oil and pay your debts. You and your sons
can live on what is left."[7]

This moment in the life of Elisha gives us so much insight into his understanding of how God works in the world. He never actually tells the woman what God is going to do; he tells her only what she needs to do. And although she feels she has nothing to offer, he reveals to her that even the little she has entrusted to God will create a future she could never imagine. Our needs are God's opportunity to reveal his generosity and goodness toward us.

The woman has a small jar of olive oil. It's amazing how God doesn't need much to do much. He just needs everything we have, which, contrary to our own self-evaluations, is very little in comparison to God. Elisha then tells her to go to her neighbors and ask for empty jars. And I love how he insists, "Don't ask for just a few." It jumps out to me that Elisha gives her a heads-up to not ask for too little. Why didn't he do the same for Jehoash? We may never know, but it does strike me that she was a poor widow and he was a powerful king. Perhaps God expects more faith of us when we have been given more. Her faith would save her life; the fate of a kingdom was at stake with the king. Elisha demanded greater faith of the king because there were greater stakes involved. He seems to know the human inclination to expect too little from God. It's as if he's trying to prod the woman's faith: "Trust me, you're going to want to have a lot of empty jars."

We don't know how many jars the widow selects or how many neighbors she asks. Maybe, out of embarrassment, she goes to just a few, or maybe she puts her humiliation aside and goes to everyone she can find and every door she can knock on. After all, she isn't asking for anything of great value. She isn't asking others to provide for her. All she wants are the empty jars. God will take what is seen as worthless to others and turn it into containers for his abundance.

And there the woman and her son begin. She takes the little bit of olive oil she has in her small jar and begins pouring it into the jars she has gathered. The oil is multiplied over and over again. She keeps pouring and pouring and pouring, and when all the jars are full, she says to her son, "Bring me another one." And he has to give her the bad news: "There is not a jar left."[8]

I imagine in that moment she wishes with every fiber of her being that she'd had greater foresight and more jars than she had collected. It is not incidental that when all the jars are full and there is not a jar left, then and only then does the oil stop flowing. God does not run out of oil; the widow runs out of empty jars. Fortunately, it is more than she needs. She is able to sell the oil and pay off her debts, making it certain that her sons will never live as slaves but will always walk as free men.

This moment in Elisha's life carries the same profound truth that we find in the moment with Jesus and the two blind men. Even though our need is obvious, there is yet the question, "What do you want?" God is trying to teach us something here. He will fill every empty jar that we bring to him. He will take the small jar of oil you have and multiply it into unimaginable abundance. And perhaps most important, when you prepare your hearts to receive from God, you shouldn't ask for just a few jars. Get all the jars you can, because the moment they're full, the oil will stop flowing.

This is not at all about greed or avarice; this is not about choosing gluttony over gratitude. This is about posturing your heart and life in God's direction, knowing that while he may not give you everything you ask for, he is the God who waits for us to ask in such a way that the provision would be proof that he is with us. We must never forget that God is the one "who is able to do immeasurably more than all we ask or imagine, according to his power that is at work within us."[9]

God can do and desires to do far more than we could ever ask for or imagine. We simply are not able to offend him by making our asks too big. In Psalm 2:8, we are told,

> Ask me,
> and I will make the nations your inheritance,
> the ends of the earth your possession.

Now, that's a big ask. It's a God-sized ask. You may have to settle in many areas of your life, but never settle for less than what God created you to live.

10

Battle Ready

I was twenty-nine years old and I was the pastor of a tiny congregation in South Dallas near the Cotton Bowl. We were one of the most violent zip codes in the United States. Our area had an extremely high crime rate and murder rate.

When I began, fewer than ten adults met together in a duplex on the very street where Aaron Spelling had lived when he was a child. We were in the shadow of the place where President John F. Kennedy was assassinated. And now neither the district attorney's office nor the probation office would allow their employees to venture into this community.

I had been there nearly six years, and an objective analysis would most likely classify me as a failure. On a good day, I preached to fifty people. Our congregation was made up of single mothers who had large families, the children usually from different fathers. The men who did join us were often drug dealers whose careers were deeply entrenched in the black market. Our congregation was comprised of African Americans, undocumented aliens, and a few Caucasians who would drive in from outside the area. Most of our congregation was on welfare, and the average education level was equivalent to that of an elementary-school student.

I spent most of my twenties walking those streets, infiltrating drug cartels, and bringing Christ to those who were invisible to most of America. I imagine that most of the johns attended churches in the suburbs, but the prostitutes came to Cornerstone. I spent nearly ten years in this environment and always found it profoundly rewarding. There was, I assure you, no fame or notoriety attached. I lived in obscurity. Even after ten years, we would consider it a miracle if three hundred people ever joined us on a Sunday.

It was August 21, 1988. I had just returned home from a week away at a camp. I was exhausted and all I wanted to do was sleep. My wife, Kim, had recruited me as a volunteer to work backstage at a huge faith-based event that she helped administrate. Twenty thousand people would gather that night in Reunion Arena, where the Dallas Mavericks played basketball. My assignment was to serve as a "directional adviser." This meant I would stand backstage and point the flashlight in the direction people should walk after they had responded to the message and were seeking further counseling.

I had served in this capacity for the past several years. I was always happy to do it, but on that day I was just too tired. I told Kim they would need to find someone else to replace me for that night. She was not cooperative. She expressed her conviction that I had given my word and that I should be there to fulfill my commitment. I pushed back and reminded her that the job did not require any real skill or talent and that my absence shouldn't even be an issue. She was relentless. I was exhausted. Having learned early the skills of marital compromise, I gave in and agreed to go.

I didn't have clean clothes, nor did I have a good attitude. I stopped by a store called Miller's Outpost and bought a pair of jeans on my way to the event. I was in such a hurry and so frustrated that I didn't bother to try on the pants or even check the size. When I got there, I put them on and realized they were several sizes too large and too long. I think it was the beginning of old-school hip-hop culture.

Less than an hour before the event, Dr. Carlos McCloud, the executive director of the conference, came to me and explained that the speaker who was scheduled was not able to make it because his plane had been delayed. For some unexplainable reason, instead of calling up a speaker from his considerable entourage, he grabbed me and said he felt that God was calling me to speak that night. Honestly, when he said it, I thought he was joking. I thought he was playing with my emotions and waiting for me to respond with an eager "Put me in, coach" so that he could come back and humble me by letting me know that would never happen.

He said it a second time, trying to get through to me the importance of this moment. I laughed and blew off his invitation once more.

The third time, he grabbed me by the shoulders, began shaking me, and put his face as close to my face as humanly possible without touching. He violated every sense of propriety and personal-space requirements. With all the conviction he could muster, he said, "Erwin, the Lord is calling you to preach tonight." The third time, it finally sunk in. I realized he wasn't joking; he wasn't mocking me—he was calling me out.

This man was thirty years older than I and we had a tenuous relationship at best. I didn't get him, and he didn't get me. He was a full-on conservative Southern Baptist who wore suits everywhere he went, and I was a preacher in blue jeans and tennis shoes. In his world everyone carried a Bible; in my world everyone carried a weapon. Did I mention I left my Bible at home? I didn't see any reason to bring it. All I would need was a flashlight, and that would be provided.

So I looked at him and said, "I'll need a Bible." He didn't let that discourage him at all. He just looked at me and said, "What translation?" and he made it happen.

I staggered away after he left me in that moment. I went and found my wife, eager to tell her what had just transpired. I thought she would be stunned, maybe paralyzed in disbelief. The moment I told her what happened, she looked at me with no surprise at all. In fact, she decided to turn this into a learning moment. She said,

"God told me you were going to preach tonight when I woke up this morning. I have known all day this was going to happen."

I was confused and asked her if someone had told her the speaker wasn't coming.

She said, "No, God told me you would be speaking."

I was a little frustrated then. After all, she was my wife. If she had this kind of insider information, she should have told me. I asked her why she didn't tell me that she had thought I was going to speak that night, and she responded as only Kim can: "Because you needed to come for the right reasons. You needed to come here to serve, to be faithful to what you had committed to. I knew, if you didn't show up, you would have missed this opportunity that God had waiting for you."

I'm not sure which conversation shook me up more.

At that point, I was less than sixty minutes away from being expected on that platform, and I felt way too small for this big moment. As I was walking backstage to secure a Bible, someone whose identity I do not remember said to me, "I just heard that you're speaking tonight. This is your moment. This is the make-or-break moment of your life."

His words were like kerosene on the fire of my insecurities. I found a small room, closed the door behind me, fell on the floor, and began praying and weeping uncontrollably. If I was going to get only one moment that would define me for the rest of my life, I would really have preferred more advance notice. It's not that I hadn't dreamed of a moment like this. It's not as if I hadn't wanted

a value that I did not perceive. The streets were the perfect training ground for what seminary could not do for me. I look back now and realize that each day when I took on the hard work of being faithful in the small things, I was being prepared for something greater than I ever could have imagined.

So many of us are trying to get "there," wherever "there" might be. But when we get there, we're not ready for it. If we take shortcuts, we're going to get there before we're ready. Whatever God has planned, we need to get prepared for it. When we finally get there, we need to be ready. We need to be ready for those unexpected moments when we're called to elevate, those moments so much bigger than we are that we can hardly breathe. We must be battle ready.

The great tragedy would be to live your life *waiting* for that moment to come instead of living your life *preparing* for when the moment comes. In God's economy, nothing is wasted. Everything you do today that seems insignificant will find its significance. You should never see any task as too small for you. If small is what you are entrusted with, that's your stewardship.

Striking the last arrow is not only about seizing every opportunity; it is also about being the right person at the right moment. The moment requires action or even reaction. Those moments and actions are informed and fueled by who we are. The best way to ensure that you will seize every opportunity is to be the best expression of who you are. Too many of us spend far too much time trying to maximize the opportunities around us and too little time committed to maximizing the potential within us. What I have seen over a lifetime is that, from our perception, we wonder why God hasn't given us the opportunities we long for, and from his perception, he wonders why we chose to be unprepared for the opportunities he placed right in front of us. Failure is rarely about the challenges we face; rather, it is about our lack of preparation. You cannot know every challenge you will face, but you can know who you are when you face that challenge!

BOTTOMS UP

One of the most interesting characters I've met in recent days is Charlie Lew. Charlie was born in Scotland and now lives in Los Angeles. His accent makes him sound as if he belongs in *Braveheart,* and he also looks the part. In college Charlie was a soccer player who later walked on in hopes to play football for Florida State University. There are very few 270-pound soccer players, but hitting people and stopping them cold seemed a natural talent for him.

After Florida State, he left Jacksonville and moved to Los Angeles while attending Loyola Law School. I know Charlie as a restaurateur. Almost walking distance from my house is a restaurant called Stout Burgers and Beer, where you can have one of the best burgers in Los Angeles. Charlie was recognized by *Los Angeles Business Journal* as the best up-and-coming restaurateur and continues to expand his creative enterprises across the country. When he decided to start Stout, he chose as his location an uninviting, dirty, and run-down coffee shop in the heart of Hollywood. With both vision and determination, he became one of the significant forces to catalyze the redevelopment of central Hollywood.

I asked Charlie how he ended up in the restaurant business, and it felt as if I were in the middle of a shell game as he told his story. His life is a series of fast and unexpected moving parts. While Charlie was trying to pay his way through law school, he worked as a security guard in one of LA's most popular clubs, called Las Palmas. While he was there, he did every job he could get his hands on. He was a busboy, a barback, and even a driver for intoxicated owners. From Las Palmas, he moved as a bodyguard through several of the Hollywood hot spots. I don't think Charlie knew while living in Scotland that studying martial arts would prepare him for this particular occupation, but it was this occupation that opened up the door for the next phase of his life.

While he was working as head of security and floor manager for a growing bar-management group, the owners suddenly found themselves in a serious legal crisis. The owner came to Charlie and told him that he needed his legal help. Charlie had never actually worked as an attorney up to that point. He was comfortable as the head of security but felt completely out of his league handling this lawsuit. He now was going to be litigating a heated land dispute.

After a brief but intense legal battle, Charlie was paid for his successful services with shares in what would become one of the most successful bar/lounges in Los Angeles's nightlife history. Charlie went from busboy to bodyguard to head of security to stockholder in a successful club. In each phase of his life, his diligence and determination helped him garner the skills and competencies necessary for the next phase of his life. It's from there that Charlie opened up his first restaurant, and from that first success, he extended his reach to as far as Austin, Texas, and Charlotte, North Carolina.

What I love about Charlie's story is that his is a journey of unexpected turns and twists. There was no straight line from a boy growing up in Scotland to a restaurateur living in Los Angeles and opening up franchises across the United States. His journey was full of unexpected challenges that he turned into opportunities. From waiting on tables at the age of sixteen to designing tables twenty years later, if you remove the middle it would look like a straight line to success. The beautiful thing is that you are not settling for less when you are waiting on tables or bagging groceries if you are doing it with all of your passion and to the best of your ability. I assure you, when you bring your best when you are at the bottom, you will rise to the top.

WITH YOUR LAST BREATH

I'm not sure what Elijah saw in Elisha—why he chose him above any other. Scripture doesn't tell us what Elijah knew about him or what he saw in him. All we learn of Elisha is how he responded when opportunity came. When Elijah called him, Elisha followed. When Elijah tried to leave him behind, Elisha refused. When they stood alone after they had crossed the Jordan, Elisha had the audacity to ask Elijah for a double portion of his spirit. Even Elijah wasn't sure if that was possible. As powerful as Elijah was, Elisha proved to be all the more.

What we know about Elisha is that the moment never seemed too big for him. He never stumbled into the future. He never had that uncomfortable uncertainty of being unprepared. Whatever else God might do or whatever else would come Elisha's way, the one thing that Elisha seemed to make sure of was that he would show up prepared. Every time he got there, he was ready.

Maybe that explains his anger toward the king when he struck the arrow only three times. These were some of the last words of Elisha before he died: "Take the arrows. . . . Strike the ground."[2] And the king, of course, struck it three times and stopped. It seemed incredible to Elisha that the king would stop. Why would anyone stop before God commands it? Why would anyone settle for a partial victory? Why would anyone settle for less? Who wouldn't strike and strike and strike until there were no arrows left?

It is not incidental that Elisha died immediately after this defining moment. The King would live knowing he settled for less. Elisha would die knowing he never settled.

This was a man who died leaving nothing undone. Yet there is a peculiar sidenote that says that long after Elisha was buried, Moabite raiders would invade the land every spring on a particular day. Some Israelites were burying a friend when suddenly they saw the band of raiders. So they threw the man's body into Elisha's tomb. "When the body touched Elisha's bones," we're told, "the man came to life and stood up on his feet."[3]

I think this is a not-so-subtle reminder that if you truly live before you die, your life will have a power that not even death can conquer. There are some of us with two feet planted squarely on the ground. We're alive, so to speak, but to be near us brings death and disappointment. Better to be like Elisha, who in physical death was still bringing life!

So what will you do? What will you choose? Will you settle for less than what God has intended for you, or will you just keep striking the arrow until there is nothing left of you to give, until you have given everything you have and everything you are and you know that, when it is all said and done, you've died with your quiver empty?

While Jesus hung on the cross, in the final minutes of his life, he uttered one word that has been translated into three: "It is finished."[4] There is no more profound example of a man who left nothing undone, who held nothing back, who gave everything of himself and gave himself completely. Though it was a tragic death, there's something strangely beautiful about that moment: being able to whisper with your last breath one word that lets the world know you did exactly what you were born to do. In that moment, death has no power, death has no victory. There is no regret—only a deep sense of fulfillment.

I am convinced that when we live our lives connected to the One who gave his life for us—when we live fearlessly, courageously, and without reservation—we will come to the end of our own lives and with our last breaths we, too, will be able to say, "Mission completed." And perhaps in that moment, we will hear Jesus whisper into the depth of our souls, "Well done, good and faithful servant!"[5]

Ralph Waldo Emerson said, "The way to write is to throw your body at the mark when your arrows are spent."[6] I agree wholeheartedly, except I would add one particular nuance: that the way to *live* is to throw your body at the mark when your arrows are spent. May we all stand on the battlefield charging fearlessly toward the enemy lines and know that when it's all said and done, we struck our last arrow.

For though I may not know you personally, this I know for certain—there are great battles ahead of you. There are dragons to slay and giants to bring down. And while you may not know what battles you are yet to face, there is one thing you can know—that you are battle ready. That you are prepared for the great fight. That for you there is no option. You will shoot your every arrow. And when your bow is done, you will take that last arrow in your hand, and with your last breath and all the strength left within you—you will strike, you will strike, and you will strike.

For additional resources, visit

www.erwinmcmanus.com

ACKNOWLEDGMENTS

The Last Arrow is in many ways a life message for me. The words that make up this book are as reflective of my philosophy of life as any I have ever written.

The writing of this book came at a time of great challenge and even turmoil in my life. There are always labor pains involved in writing a book, but this time the struggle was called cancer. Yet it was as if we never missed a beat as we stayed true to our commitment to finish the book on time. As always, it took a great team to pull it all together. I am grateful to each and every person who made this project possible and especially to those who so believe in its message that you have given your time and energy to make it a success.

I want to thank the Fedd Agency and especially Esther Fedorkevich and Whitney Gossett for believing in me and the message of *The Last Arrow*. Your passion and commitment to this message have been inspiring to me and have fueled me to believe that great things will result from all our hard work.

I also wish to acknowledge the team at WaterBrook for making this book possible and getting the message out across the world. Thank you, Alex Field and Andrew Stoddard, for all your hard work and commitment to *The Last Arrow.*

From my team here in LA, I must always give thanks for Holly Quillen and Alisah Duran, who are more important to me than pen and paper is to a writer. None of this would happen without you two. Also thanks to Brooke Odom for helping me with so many of the amazing interviews that add so much color to the manuscript.

Thank you as well to Deborah Giarratana, who has given so much of herself to expand the influence and impact of this message.

I also want to thank my leadership team at Mosaic in Los Angeles, who makes it possible for me to carve out time to write and create such works as *The Last Arrow.* There is no place or people like Mosaic, and I am so grateful to call you my family and my church. You are the tribe I walk with every day. You are the warriors who fight the great fight with me side by side. Together we have faced great challenges and fought great battles! You have redefined for me the meaning of church, and I could not imagine doing life without you. Thank you for believing in me and my message and believing that the world needs to hear what we have learned in the struggle.

I want to thank my beautiful wife, Kim, who has stayed at my side for more than thirty-three years. You have seen me at my worst and at my best. I know you had to face the prospect of living life without me this year. I could not do this without you. We carry each other forever in our hearts. You are a hurricane and a tempest. The world is never the same where you have traveled. Your arrow flies to the most remote and dangerous places in the world doing good that changes the lives of the nameless. I am honored to be your husband.

I want to express my love and affection for the child God gave us before we had children: Paty. I am so grateful that God brought you into our lives. To Paty Campodonico; her husband, Steve; and their beautiful children, Stevie and Mia. I am so proud of you. I celebrate your lives and the love you have for Jesus and for people. The future is waiting for you. May you pursue it with all your hearts and strength. May you live fully and fearlessly for the cause of Christ.

I want to thank my daughter, Mariah, for personifying what it means to give all of oneself for the sake of Christ and the church. You are the wind and waves that move oceans to their shores. Thank you for leading the way. Thank you for your sacrifice. Thank you for your fire and passion. You are what a heart wholly given to God looks like. You are both a source of grace and a force of nature. You are an arrow flying true. It was both beautiful and painful to give you away in marriage this year. You have married well. Jake Goss is a man's man and a man after God's own heart. I love Jake and could not be happier that the Goss family is now our family as well. Jake, I am proud of you and honored to have you as a son.

To my son, Aaron, who is passion wrapped up in skin. You

have returned to us with a fire that burns hot and bright. You were made for the front lines. You were born for the battle. You bleed for the cause. You are a son of thunder. You are both arrow and archer. I love doing life together and fighting battles together.

I would like to express my gratitude to the doctors and surgeons who cared for me and saw me through to health and new life: Dr. Ramin Khalili, Dr. Kenneth Lam, Dr. Lisa Ma, Dr. Se-Young Lee, and Dr. Sandy Lee.

I would also like to express my gratitude to Brad and Shanda Damphousse for their investment in our mission and their deep passion for getting the message out to as many people as possible. Thank you so much for filling our quiver with more arrows than we ever imagined.

Most of all, I must thank the One who died for me and taught me how to live. Thank you, Jesus, for giving all of yourself on our behalf. Thank you for showing me the way to life. Jesus, you have proved to be everything you've ever promised. You are truly the Last Arrow.

NOTES

Chapter 1: The Point of No Return

1. See 2 Kings 13:14–20.
2. *Gattaca,* directed by Andrew Niccol (Culver City, CA: Columbia Pictures, 1997), DVD.

Chapter 2: Save Nothing for the Next Life

1. Mick Fanning, quoted in Nick Mulvenney, "Shaken Fanning Not Giving Up on Surfing Despite Shark Attack," Sports News, *Reuters,* July 21, 2015, http://uk .reuters.com/article/uk-surfing-australia-fanning -idUKKCN0PV0M020150721.
2. Devdutt Pattanaik, "East Vs. West—the Myths That Mystify," TEDIndia, 18:26, filmed November 2009, www.ted.com/speakers/devdutt_pattanaik.
3. 2 Kings 13:19.

Chapter 3: Choose the Future

1. 1 Kings 19:20.
2. See 2 Kings 13:18–19.

3. Acts 7:3.

4. Luke 9:57–62.

5. Luke 14:26.

6. Erwin Raphael McManus, *Chasing Daylight: Seize the Power of Every Moment* (Nashville: Thomas Nelson, 2002).

Chapter 4: Set Your Past on Fire

1. Jeremiah 20:9.

Chapter 5: Refuse to Stay Behind

1. See 2 Kings 2:1–10.

2. 2 Kings 2:11–15.

3. John 19:30.

4. Isaiah 6:8.

Chapter 6: Act Like Your Life Depends on It

1. Luke 24:5.

2. 2 Kings 7:3–4.

3. 2 Kings 7:5–8.

4. 2 Kings 7:9.

5. Jeremiah 29:11. See other promises in Deuteronomy 5:33; 8:18; 28:11; 30:9; Psalm 1:3; Proverbs 28:25; Malachi 3:10; Mark 10:29–30; Luke 6:38; John 10:10; 2 Corinthians 9:8; Philippians 4:19; 3 John 2.

Chapter 7: Stand Your Ground

1. See 2 Samuel 23:11–12.

2. See Ecclesiastes 1:2.

3. Isaiah 43:18–19.

4. Revelation 21:5; see Ezekiel 36:26; 2 Corinthians 5:17; Psalm 96:1; Lamentations 3:22–23.

5. Erwin Raphael McManus, *The Artisan Soul: Crafting Your Life into a Work of Art* (New York: HarperCollins, 2014).

Chapter 8: Find Your People

1. Erwin Raphael McManus, *The Barbarian Way: Unleash the Untamed Faith Within* (Nashville: Thomas Nelson, 2005).

2. See 1 Samuel 20:1–15.

3. 1 Samuel 20:4.

4. 1 Samuel 20:17.

5. See 2 Samuel 23:8–39.

6. Ruth 1:16.

7. Ruth 1:17.

8. Ecclesiastes 4:9–12.

Chapter 9: Know What You Want

1. Jim Blanchard Leadership Forum, Leadership Institute, Columbus State University, https://jblf.columbusstate.edu.

2. Matthew 20:30–32.

3. Matthew 20:33–34.

4. See Psalm 37:4.

5. 2 Kings 4:1.

6. 2 Kings 4:2.

7. 2 Kings 4:3–7.

8. 2 Kings 4:6.

9. Ephesians 3:20.

Chapter 10: Battle Ready

1. See Luke 16:10.

2. 2 Kings 13:18.

3. 2 Kings 13:21.

4. John 19:30.

5. Matthew 25:21.

6. Ralph Waldo Emerson, quoted in Robert D. Richardson, *First We Read, Then We Write: Emerson on the Creative Process* (Iowa City, IA: University of Iowa Press, 2009), xii.